Social influences

This comprehensive textbook explores areas of human behaviour as diverse as mob violence, the need to obey, gender behaviour, and the behaviour of groups and their leaders. *Social Influences* is firmly within the discipline of social psychology and deals with topics such as obedience, conformity, independent behaviour, crowd behaviour, group behaviour and leadership. Enlivened with contemporary case studies and examples and giving regular reviews of important theories and studies, it will be essential reading to students studying social influences at the introductory level.

Kevin Wren is a Moderator and Examiner for A-level Psychology. He is a freelance lecturer in psychology and runs a private practice working with special needs children.

Routledge Modular Psychology

Series editors: Cara Flanagan is the Assessor for the Associated Examining Board (AEB) and an experienced A-level author. Kevin Silber is Senior Lecturer in Psychology at Staffordshire University. Both are A-level examiners in the UK.

The *Routledge Modular Psychology* series is a completely new approach to introductory level psychology, tailor-made to the new modular style of teaching. Each short book covers a topic in more detail than any large textbook can, allowing teacher and student to select material exactly to suit any particular course or project.

The books have been written especially for those students new to higher-level study, whether at school, college or university. They include specially designed features to help with technique, such as a model essay at an average level with an examiner's comments to show how extra marks can be gained. The authors are all examiners and teachers at the introductory level.

The *Routledge Modular Psychology* texts are all user-friendly and accessible and include the following features:

- practice essays with specialist commentary to show how to achieve a higher grade
- chapter summaries to assist with revision
- progress and review exercises
- glossary of key terms
- summaries of key research
- further reading to stimulate ongoing study and research
- website addresses for additional information
- cross-referencing to other books in the series

Also available in this series (titles listed by syllabus section):

Social influences

Kevin Wren

London and New York

First published 1999
by Routledge
11 New Fetter Lane, London EC4P 4EE

Simultaneously published in the USA and Canada
by Routledge
29 West 35th Street, New York, NY 10001

Routledge is an imprint of the Taylor & Francis Group

© 1999 Kevin Wren

Typeset in Times by Routledge
Printed and bound in Great Britain by
St Edmundsbury Press, Bury St Edmunds, Suffolk

British Library Cataloguing in Publication Data
A catalogue record for this book is available from the British Library

Library of Congress Cataloging in Publication Data
Wren, Kevin, 1947–
(Routledge modular psychology)
Includes bibliographical references and index.
1. Social influence. I. Title. II. Series.
HM1176.W74 1999
303.3'4–dc21   99–12797

ISBN 0–415–18658–7 (hbk)
ISBN 0–415–18659–5 (pbk)

Contents

Acknowledgements

I hope you enjoy reading about social influences as much as I enjoy thinking about and teaching the subject. I should like to take this opportunity to thank my students both past and present for their attention and on occasions for candid remarks which have often stopped me in my thought process to ponder further some moot point. I would like to thank Paul Rookes and Kevin Silber for encouraging me to embark on this project and Cara Flanagan for her suggestions and revisions. Viv Ward and Moira Taylor of Routledge have been very helpful and supportive and deserve my thanks. I must not forget a long-standing friend, John Cowsill, for the many suggestions and examples he gave me. Finally, I should like to thank John Kirkwood for his wit and intellect and the many long discussions we had about current trends in psychology.

The series editors and Routledge acknowledge the expert help of Paul Humphreys, Examiner and Reviser for A-level Psychology, in compiling the Study Aids section of each book in the series.

They also acknowledge the Associated Examining Board (AEB) for granting permission to use their examination material. The AEB do not accept responsibility for the answers or examiner comment in the Study Aids chapter of this book or any other book in the series.

Introduction

Imagine sitting at home on a cold, windy night. Winter is dragging on and despite the few rays of sun, the day has been like many others: dark, dull, rainy and tiring. It's nearly nine-thirty and you're in your night clothes with a cup of a hot milk sat in front of the TV. There's some benign comedy programme on but you are not taking too much notice of it because you are tired and beginning to get sleepy. The phone rings and your flat mate shouts, 'It's for you sleepy head.'

'Uh,' you mumble down the phone.

'Hi. Get yourself moving it's time to party.' It is your good friend with a few of the others from the office.

'Too tired,' you mumble.

'Come on you old so-and-so, live a little. It's Friday night. No one stays in on a Friday.'

You whine about being worn out, but your friend is having none of it.

'We'll be round with the gang in about an hour. Be ready.'

'But ... '

'One hour.' And the phone goes down.

'I'm not going,' you tell yourself.

'Don't be so boring,' shouts your flat mate. 'Get your gear on and go. Come on, everyone's out tonight.'

'Not you as well,' you moan.

'Well everyone who's got a life, that is.'

Three hours later at the disco you win the 'Silly Dance' competition and have found yourself an interesting potential partner for the rest of the evening. You are now talkative, charming and the life and soul of the party.

Why did this change occur in someone so lethargic? What has happened to change them so radically? A social psychologist would say '**social influences**'. The mere presence of other people can have a profound effect on our behaviour. They do not have to be people we know, as in the above example. We may never have even met the person but just the thought of someone else's views may influence us. Despite the brevity of the example given, social psychologists would point to a number of aspects which demonstrate the idea that within a society or group we are influencing others and in turn being influenced by them.

We all like to think we are unique. In fact our parents, lovers and friends often tell us so when being endearing. When you look at the factors that go to influence our behaviour, e.g. genetics, environment and chance, you might well agree that no two people could ever be alike. Social psychologists agree with this but they would also point to behaviour which regularly occurs throughout a society and has a high degree of uniformity, e.g. **audience** behaviour at a pop concert, queuing for a bus, or conforming to our boss's opinions about how we work. They would say that in this respect, i.e. when acting as a **group** of individuals, we are not always as unique as we think we are. In this book I am going to look at a number of aspects of behaviour where our public self is involved. I hope to show that despite the variety of backgrounds, life experiences and inherited characteristics we have, our behaviour is frequently a result of others being there, i.e. it is due to social influences.

If we re-examine the example above some of the ways in which we influence each other are quite subtle. The suggestion that everyone is out on a Friday night is an example, in so far as it implies that not going out is odd. This suggestion is often used by advertisers to convince customers to buy their products, e.g.'90% of all ... owners buy ...'. The conversation also highlights the influence of social norms, i.e. expectations and rules that influence what we ought to think and how we ought to behave; if one has 'got a life, that is'. At the extreme these norms can influence and maintain individuals within a whole political ideology, e.g. Nazi Germany or the Soviet Union. Social norms (influence), therefore, are important in helping us to explain many aspects of human social interaction.

Most of us take these influences and expectations for granted, probably because they are so subtle. It is only when we feel forced into behaving in a way that contravenes our personal morality that we come face to face with social influence, such as finding ourselves part of a rioting crowd.

In this book, therefore, we are going to examine social influences such as conformity, obedience and collective behaviour. Some of the case studies and examples we will look at are shocking, some will be examples of behaviour we can all identify with and others will be unique sets of circumstances only a very few of us will ever encounter in a lifetime.

Obedience

Introduction
Obedience research
Milgram's experiment
Criticisms of Milgram's experiment
Other obedience studies
Field experiments
Some explanations of obedience
Summary

Introduction

One aspect of behaviour brought about through social influence is **obedience**, i.e. obeying direct instructions or orders. As car drivers we obey the signals directed at us by traffic police, e.g. to turn or slow down. School pupils respond to the instructions directed at them by their teachers and as soldiers we obey the orders of our commanding officers. In some situations our obedience is taken for granted and in turn we seldom question our own obedience, e.g. responding to the instructions of health workers and carers. As with other aspects of human behaviour it has been the destructive, rather than the constructive, aspects of behaviour that has commanded the attention of both psychologists and non-psychologists alike.

Obedience research

It would be considered unethical to perform an experiment to investigate the obedience behaviour of soldiers during situations such as the Holocaust of World War II. We are left, therefore, with few alternatives other than to rely on the eyewitness evidence of people like Holocaust victims. The problem with this type of evidence is that very often these participants are psychologically and physically damaged by their experiences. Eitinger and Støm's study (1973) of ex-concentration camp inmates revealed a higher than normal incidence of both physical and psychological illness. Similarly, interviews with those who perpetrated the violence are difficult, with interviewees being deliberately uncooperative or being very selective in what they wish to remember (Browning, 1992).

Milgram's response to reading about incidents such as described above was to conduct a number of experiments to investigate destructive obedience. He wanted to investigate whether some individuals or cultures are simply more obedient than others, or whether everyone is obedient in certain situations. If so, what are the key elements of these situations?

Milgram's experiment

His baseline experiment is described in article 1 of the key research summaries in chapter 6. (Read this now.)

Milgram's original experiment demonstrated clearly, and shockingly, that ordinary individuals are obedient. He conducted a further eighteen experiments in which he varied some of the parameters in order to investigate further the situational factors which might have produced such a significant result. In all but one of the variants the participants were male, non-graduates between 20 and 50 years of age. In one other study, in which females were the participants, he found a similar level of obedience.

These were some of the key findings:

- The presence of another/others who are seen to disobey the experimenter reduces the level of obedience. In the case of two disobedient participants, obedience rates dropped to 10%.

(Demonstrating the influence of **group pressure**: in this case positively.)

- The closeness of the teacher to the learner increased the likeliness of disobedience in so far as when the 'learner' was visible obedience rates dropped to 40%.
- Obedience was less likely if the experimenter was not in the room but issued orders over a phone link. When the experimenter was absent, teachers often administered shocks of a lower dosage than ordered.
- Re-locating the experiment from Yale University to a less prestigious office had some impact on the results in that obedience rates dropped from 65% to 48%.
- When participants were placed in the role of bystander to another's obedience, 93% remained on task and did not intervene.
- A small reduction in obedience rates was observed when the participants and the experimenter agreed prior to the experiment to release participants if requested. The experimenter subsequently ignored this agreement.

A very interesting variant was where obedience to authority was demonstrated to have a beneficial effect. In a series of trials the learner demanded that the experiment continued despite indicating obvious pain on the pretext that he wanted to show that he could 'take' the punishment. When the experimenter ordered the teacher to stop, they obeyed instantly. This seems to show that people continue to obey authority for good or evil and further supports the major influence of an authority figure.

Milgram's (1963, 1965, 1974) basic study and variations demonstrate that obedience is dependent on intricate situational factors. Participants who would harm another under the direct orders of an authority figure (the experimenter) would be able to disobey the experimenter if with a defiant co-participant, or if the experimenter had left the room.

The implications of Milgram's baseline condition and many of the variations are best expressed in Milgram's own words:

if an anonymous experimenter could successfully command adults to subdue a fifty-year-old man, and force on him painful electric shocks against his protests, one can only wonder what government, with its vastly greater authority and prestige, can command of its subjects.

(Milgram, 1965: 75)

Progress exercise

Answer the following either verbally or in written note form.

1 Briefly outline Milgram's baseline experiment.
2 Why were Milgram's results so surprising?
3 List three situational factors Milgram changed in subsequent experiments.
4 In relation to 3, describe the results of these studies and what they seem to tell us about destructive obedience?

Criticisms of Milgram's experiment

Ecological validity

Milgram's studies have been questioned on the grounds of **ecological validity**. In research it is important that the claims you make for an experiment and the data generated actually examine what you say they examine. Thomas Kuhn (1962), a scientist, historian and philosopher, says that modern science experiments only show what modern scientists claim they show. In other words all experiments can be questioned on the grounds that they do not really test what the experimenter claims the experiment tests. In the case of Milgram, therefore, is his study an examination of destructive obedience such as was witnessed in real-world examples like Auschwitz, an example of Nazi obedience? There is not always a simple 'yes it does'/ 'no it doesn't' answer to this question. Many social psychologists have noted the different quality of human relationships in real life and in a laboratory. What we may be seeing in a social science laboratory experiment is only what happens in a laboratory and therefore it is difficult to generalise from the laboratory results to real life. In this case, the laboratory experiment is said to lack ecological validity. Others point out that limiting variables so that they can be manipulated and measured easily is not comparable with real-world situations such as German concentration or death camps. Briefly, anecdotal evidence (Wiesel, 1958; Levi, 1986) and evidence from social scientists (Cohen, 1954) indicate that Auschwitz was a complex society, as well as an infamous Nazi death camp. As a large collection of individuals, therefore, it developed its own unique set of social norms and values. Many would say that to try and emulate this or part of it, i.e. destructive obedience, in a laboratory setting would mean that many significant features of the 'real' situation are lost.

Internal validity

But studies can be invalid for other reasons, such as the way in which data was collected or the behaviour of the experimenter. This is called internal validity.

Rosenthal (1966), Orne and Holland (1968) and others have demonstrated the effects of **demand characteristics**. These are features of the experimental procedure or setting which bias results. An example of this would be an experimenter who, as a result of a poorly designed set of standard instructions, invited participants to behave in a particular way or who recruited participants from a sample which was not random.

In relation to the above, two aspects of Milgram's procedure have come in for criticism:

- The fact that Milgram paid his 'volunteers' and recruited them via a newspaper advertisement is not considered to be random sampling.
- The experimenter contradicted his participants both verbally and non-verbally on a number of occasions, such as by telling participants that a shock of 345 volts would not cause tissue damage when the switch was clearly labelled as very dangerous.

On these alone, some psychologists would condemn Milgram's results as internally invalid.

Ethics

These experiments are unethical to the point that they probably would not be sanctioned today. Bruno Bettelheim described them as 'vile' and went on to say that they were of little worth. Today's **APA** and **BPS** guidelines, for example, state clearly that:

- At all times a participant's full and informed consent must be obtained prior to the start of an experiment.
- The participant must be at liberty to withdraw at any time.
- The participant's health and mental well-being must be safe-guarded.

Milgram's experimental procedures seem to have broken all three of the above guidelines. His own description of one of his participants 20 minutes into the experiment seems to contravene at least two:

> he was reduced to a twitching stuttering wreck who was rapidly approaching a state of nervous collapse. He constantly pulled on his earlobes, and twisted his hands. At one point he pushed his fist into his forehead and muttered: 'Oh God, let's stop it.'

Counter-arguments

Milgram felt that his debriefing procedure, involving a friendly recon-ciliation with the victim (actor), was sufficiently thorough to ensure that each participant left the laboratory 'in a state of well-being'. In a follow-up study Milgram, assisted by a psychiatrist, discovered that very few participants felt they were harmed by their experiences. Only 1.3% of participants felt that they were sorry or very sorry to have taken part in the experiment, whereas 83.7% were glad to have taken part (Milgram, 1974). Even so, modern psychologists would say that Milgram's efforts to obtain naïve participants were unethical because the participants were not fully informed and every opportunity was taken to persuade the participant to continue when some were clearly apprehensive.

On the other side of the debate, social psychologists like Elms (1982) have described such research as 'morally significant'. He feels the risks were worth taking in order to investigate a very contentious aspect of behaviour. Others would say that we could not turn our back on aspects of human behaviour just because they are distasteful and are difficult to investigate. And as Aronson (1995) observed: 'the ethics of any experiment may be less open to question when the results tell us something pleasant or flattering about human nature, and more open to question when they tell us something we'd rather not know.'

Progress exercise

Answer the following either verbally or in written note form.

1 Summarise the ethical concerns that Milgram's study brought into focus.
2 Summarise some of the points listed above which were criticisms of Milgram's procedure.

Other obedience studies

Cross-cultural studies

Since Milgram's original study and despite the ethical issues it raised there have been many variations of his baseline experiment conducted in other countries and cultures including Austria, Australia, Britain, Germany, Italy, Jordan, the Netherlands and Spain. On inspection though, the majority have been performed in predominantly 'Western' societies. They have produced a range of results, e.g. from over 90% obedience in Spain and the Netherlands to a low of 16% in Australian females. It must be pointed out that not all the studies were exact replications and therefore cannot be seen as wholly confirming Milgram's results. On the other hand, the various replications seem to generally reflect the range of scores Milgram obtained (Miller, 1986). I will examine two, a study of children by Shanab and Yahya (1977) and a part replication study conducted by Kilham and Mann (1974) in Australia.

Shanab and Yahya studied Jordanian children between the ages of 6 and 16 years. The experimenter was female. The results of the experiment showed that 73% of children administered the maximum shock to same-gender peers. This is an important variation since it seems to show that gender may well be a factor in how we behave in a situation where we are 'expected' to behave in a destructive way. This study represents an 11% increase in the levels of obedience Milgram obtained with adults. This seems to confirm the reality that children are very obedient. In the light of the number of children, past and present, who have played and are playing an active part in warfare, it is worrying. In recent history children have been implicated in war crimes, e.g. as fighters for the Khmer Rouge in Cambodia and in the recent civil war in Rwanda. However, it is difficult to generalise too much from this study since the cultures of Jordan, Rwanda and the West are very different.

The Australian study was a modified version of the Milgram baseline study involving 63 male and 62 female, first-year psychology students. The researchers wanted to examine whether there would be any difference between executive behaviour, i.e. issuing an order, and carrying out the order. Participants were either to:

1   order another to inflict pain, or
2   implement the order to inflict pain.

The researchers found obedience levels were higher in the former than the latter condition. Overall levels of obedience were lower than those reported by Milgram. Interestingly, females were less obedient than males, especially when required to carry out an order to inflict pain. Kilham and Mann explained this on the premise that females inflicting pain on another female on the orders of a male (perceived to be unreasonable) may engender concern for the other female victim. This study demonstrates two things: (i) that there may be a qualitative difference between *ordering* destructive behaviour and *carrying out* destructive behaviour; (ii) there may be gender differences in the way males and females respond. One has to ask, though, how naïve a first-year psychology graduate would be?

Field experiments

Hofling *et al.* (1966) wanted to discover if nurses would ignore the direct instructions of an unfamiliar doctor (authority figure) and conducted an interesting naturalistic study. Each nurse was instructed by a doctor by telephone to find an unauthorised drug (not on the ward list). On obtaining the drug each nurse noticed that the doctor's prescribed dose was well over the dose recommended on the label. On the orders of the doctor, but in contravention of strict hospital regulations and routines, e.g. medication could not be authorised by telephone, 20 of the 21 nurses began to prepare the medicine to give to the patient. At this point a confederate of the experimenter approached them and the process was stopped. On being debriefed the nurses complained that they were normally expected to 'obey' doctors, i.e. their medical superiors. They commented also that if they questioned a doctor's judgement it was often met with annoyance, so too were attempts to perform their duties 'by the book'.

Another experiment conducted by Bushman (1984) had his confederates dressed in either a uniform, tidy formal dress or in a worn and untidy outfit. They stood next to a person fumbling for change for a parking meter. As people passed by the confederate ordered them to give the fumbler change for the meter. In 70% of cases the passers-by obliged the uniformed confederate demonstrating that unquestioned obedience, in the majority, can be achieved merely with the symbol of authority, i.e. a uniform.

Evaluation

Both of these studies have greater ecological validity than Milgram's laboratory studies in so far as they were carried out in a real environment. However, field experiments can have flaws, which can invalidate results. Assuming that a passing group of the general public is a random sample can be one such flaw. Samples of the general public are notorious for being biased through confounding and extraneous variables. These can be as varied as the weather, the time of day, the environment the study took place in and whether, unbeknown to the researchers, the study took place in the vicinity of a public building such as a school. It can be difficult also to control variables in field studies in the same way you can in a laboratory. In Bushman's experiment, for example, it would have been very difficult to control the experiences of the participants prior to their contact with the uniformed confederate. It could be in the case of some that they may have come in contact with another uniformed official just prior to their contact with the confederate. The latter could have a bearing on how they behaved in the study.

Answer the following either verbally or in written note form.

1 Briefly describe either Hofling *et al.*'s or Bushman's study and compare them with one another.
2 What do these studies add to our understanding of destructive obedience?

Some explanations of obedience

Milgram's agentic theory

How then do we explain Milgram's results and the confirmation of them by others such as Bushman?

Milgram sought to explain them from a sociocultural perspective by claiming that we tend live in a hierarchy, i.e. a society based on the idea that individuals are ranked in terms of their power and importance. In turn, this creates a socially obedient environment. If you think of socially significant others in our world such as parents, teachers, policemen and supervisors, for example, we are often expected to obey them without question. They in turn come to expect to be obeyed. Authority figures like doctors are part of powerful, and in some cases, authoritarian collectives such as schools and hospitals. At the same time, we are encouraged to be independent, self-serving and autonomous.

Milgram proposed that we have two states of consciousness: the **agentic state** and the **autonomous state**. In the latter state we are aware of the consequences of our actions and therefore voluntarily engage in or disengage from behaviour. In the agentic state individuals see themselves as agents of others, i.e. as subordinates in an otherwise hierarchical system, and as a result they lose those aspects of themselves we might call individuality. Adolf Eichmann is a classic 'real life' example of this in so far as at his trial he pleaded, like other Nazis at the Nuremburg trials, that he was only obeying orders. In fact, he claimed, he was not the 'monster' the media of the day had painted him to be. Arendt (1963) remarked on Eichmann's 'ordinariness'. She found no violent anti-Semitism and neither did this surface in his trial. Browning (1992), a social historian, who examined pre-trial verbatim interrogations, along with other trial material of members of Reserve Police Battalion 101 (a police unit charged with keeping order in territory conquered by the German regular army), comments also that despite being professional killers many of these men did not have a history of anti-Semitic violence or criminality. Browning reports that only a quarter of the men were Nazi Party members. They seemed at the outset of the war to be 'ordinary men', e.g. barbers, clerks, metalworkers, salesmen, etc. Milgram's agentic theory therefore could account for this transition from seemingly ordinary Germans to the war criminals portrayed in films such as *Schindler's List*. As 'ordinary' Germans they were autonomous in so far as they were independent and made their own decisions. As members of the SS they were agentic in so far as they were subordinate to their officers and military discipline. They were no longer 'metalworker Bremerhaven' but *Ordnungspolizei* (security police) attached to the invading German army and charged with holding in check occupied land.

Psychoanalytic explanations

In the past many have tried to explain the murderous behaviour of war criminals such as members of Battalion 101 as being a result of **denial**. In order to defend oneself against the full horrors of what is happening individuals utilise a **defence mechanism**. According to Freud, denial is an aspect of the pleasure principle, i.e. painful perceptions are denied as part of a hallucinatory wish-fulfilment. Put another way, it is more pleasant to pretend everything is 'rosy in the garden' than admit to the full horror of what is actually happening.

In the case of Milgram's participants denying that the painful experiences of the 'learner' were really happening could have lessened the anxiety of the situation.

Is it possible for so many individuals to be using the same defence behaviour? A Freudian would probably say yes. Freudians understand that defence mechanisms come into operation automatically as a response to anxiety and in defence of the **ego**. It is natural, therefore, for individuals to defend themselves against anxiety, as a failure to do so leads to neurosis or other forms of mental illness.

Graduated commitment

Another aspect of Milgram's experiments was that the participant's involvement was graduated, i.e. their involvement was over a number of trials, not all of them anxiety provoking. Early trials involved mild electric shocks interspersed with the learner getting some of the questions correct. By the time the 'learner' began to complain decisively, the participant was 'committed'. Such gradual commitment, whereby the longer it lasts the more difficult it is to withdraw, has been noted by Freedman and Fraser (1966). They call it the **foot-in-the-door** effect. If you can get individuals to **comply**, i.e. overtly conform to the wishes of another, with a small, relatively harmless act (get your foot in the door), they feel committed. It is not difficult to get them to make the next step, e.g. to comply with a similar but more serious or important request, and so on. This technique is practised on us in our daily lives quite often. You enter a store and are approached by a sales person. They ask you to look at the merchandise and you agree (small request and a foot-in-the-door). They then ask if they can take it out of the box so that you can hold it and you agree (a larger request). The sales person then holds it up to your jacket or trousers and asks if you would like to try it on. You agree (a slightly larger request but still reasonable). All the time you are experiencing a graduated commitment.

In relation to **totalitarian** organisations such as the Third Reich, with all its bureaucracy, careerism, favouritism and militarism, it is not surprising that individuals, 'ordinary men', soon reached positions where their commitment translated into destructive obedience, i.e. carrying out of immoral orders (war crimes). During the post-war era, such individuals were identified and spoken of as 'Schreibtischtäter', literally 'desk criminals' (Lifton, 1986). These were individuals who because of their status and power ordered others, such as lower-ranking doctors or soldiers, to carry out inhuman acts.

Deindividuation

Zimbardo (1973) conducted a study of prisoner–guard behaviour (see article 4 of the key research summaries in chapter 6). Guards behaved aggressively while prisoners were apathetic. Zimbardo felt that a number of aspects had influenced the behaviour of the participants:

- Uniforms resulted in the **deindividuation** of the participants, i.e. uniforms can bring about **anonymity** and a consequent lack of personal awareness.
- Roles within society bring with them expectations regarding attitudes and values.

This seems to demonstrate that social roles can have a powerful influence over our behaviour. Guards have authority and 'expect' to be obeyed. The role expectation of a prisoner is that of obedience. The study does not just show that prisoners obeyed guards but that the participants in the study were obedient also to their social roles, which in turn were reinforced by 'uniforms'.

Authoritarian personality

Theodor Adorno *et al.* (1950) felt that personality rather than situational and environmental factors could explain obedience. They proposed that there was such a thing as an **authoritarian personality**, i.e. a person who favours an authoritarian social system and in particular admires obedience to authority figures. They piloted and developed a questionnaire, which they called the **F-scale** (F for fascism). Adorno argued that deep-seated personality traits predisposed some individuals to be highly sensitive to totalitarian and antidemocratic ideas and therefore were prone to be highly prejudicial. The evidence they gave to support this conclusion included:

- case studies, e.g. Nazis
- psychometric testing (use of the F-scale)
- situational and constitutional factors in the backgrounds of participants who scored highly on the F-scale. Clinical interviews with the latter revealed situational aspects of their childhood, such as the fact that they had been brought up by very strict parents or guardians, which were not always found in the backgrounds of low scorers.

Adorno *et al.* felt that authoritarian traits, as identified by the F-Scale, predispose some individuals towards 'fascistic' characteristics such as:

- **ethnocentrism**, i.e. the tendency to favour one's own ethnic group
- obsession with rank and status
- respect for and submissiveness to authority figures
- preoccupation with power and toughness.

In other words, the Eichmans of this world are there because they have authoritarian personalities and therefore are predisposed to cruelty, as a result of up-bringing, nature or both.

As an explanation this is in opposition to the idea that 'ordinary men', as a result of social influences, can be persuaded or driven to great acts of destructive obedience. This can not account for all those participants in obedience experiments. Browning makes the point that in Battalion 101 there were two types of men: ordinary men driven to acts of destruction by social forces; and self-selected individuals who, as Adorno implies, may have readily been disposed to Nazism and extreme racism. In other words, the authoritarian explanation can explain some but not all instances of obedience.

'Sleepers'

Steiner (1980) and Staub (1989) offer an alternative to Adorno *et al.*'s **type and trait** approach by merging this with situational factors – organisational, cultural and sociopolitical. Steiner suggests that some members of the SS and Gestapo were 'sleepers' – individuals with aggressive and prejudicial feelings. In peacetime they remain dormant, or they may have a history of being, say, wife-beaters, disgruntled or pessimistic. They rarely come to the attention of the civil courts as they curb their aggression and racial hatred. But, once a sub-culture of violence, such as the Brown Shirts, becomes legitimised this acts as an incentive and allows them to vent their violent potential. Staub goes even further and asserts that evil arising out of 'normal' individuals is the 'norm, not the exception'. For Staub the 'sleeper' is the norm, and most of us are predisposed to commit atrocities, given the 'right' circumstances.

Binding forces

Finally I should like to present one more explanation of destructive obedience, which has its roots in compliance. One could hypothesise that in an ambiguous or novel situation we often look to others for guidance. If one of these others is a significant authority figure and we do not have the time or the ability to contemplate our actions carefully the likely result will be to bow to the perceived legitimate power of the authority figure and all that they represent. The My Lai massacre in the Vietnam War serves as a real-world example. On the express orders of Lieutenant Calley, US infantrymen killed 300 unarmed Vietnamese villagers. The words of one of those who participated in the massacre is an example of the power of **binding forces**:

Q: Why did you do it?

A: Why did I do it? Because I felt like I was ordered to do it, and it seemed like that, at the time I felt like I was doing the right thing, because, like I said, I lost buddies.

Kelman and Hamilton (1989) have described the role of binding forces in these incidents. They define binding forces as 'those elements of the situation that psychologically tie the individual to the authority's definition of the situation'. These forces are reinforced by the presence of other situational factors such as peer-group pressure, being observed, chain of command, ambiguity of the situation, the presence of an authority figure, and the possible aversive consequences of disobedience. One member of Battalion 101 spoke of being called a 'weakling' by his peers for trying to evade taking part in the execution of Jews. Another spoke of not wanting to appear 'too weak' or 'cowardly' in front of his comrades despite the fact that many were uneasy about their actions.

Kelman and Hamilton suggest also that in such situations an individual's behaviour is influenced by **rule** and **role orientation**. Rule orientation is described as increasing ties to authority figures, out of a sense of powerlessness as a result of the loss of individual power, which can happen when you become part of a very disciplined group such as in a military situation. Rule-bound individuals find it very difficult to challenge authority figures because of their submissiveness. They accept, therefore, without question the authority's definition of the situation.

Role orientation is based on the idea that roles bring with them expectations and specify functional aspects of behaviour, e.g. soldiers and policemen are expected to obey and carry out orders issued by their superiors. In turn they expect to be obeyed by those they are directing or policing.

But let us not forget that obedience is a force for good as well as evil when it takes the form of constructive obedience. Throughout our daily lives we obey our doctors, take orders from health and safety personnel about how to behave in our working environment, obey commands of the emergency and security personnel, and respond to the authority of our moral and religious leaders. In this way, we remain healthy, safe and to some extent may be at peace with ourselves. In this respect, obedience is useful since it adds to our mental and physical well-being; i.e. it has survival value.

Progress exercise

Answer the following either verbally or in written note form:

1 Describe Milgram's agentic theory.
2 Explain the Freudian concept of denial, and how it helps us explain destructive obedience.
3 Describe one other explanation for destructive obedience.

Summary

Milgram investigated destructive obedience and found a high level of obedience in his participants, despite lay and professional predictions to the contrary. Milgram varied the situational parameters he thought might have added to the high level of obedience, e.g. proximity of the 'learner' to the 'teacher'. Replications seem to obtain similar results. He has been criticised on the grounds of both ethics and validity. Explanations of his results include: Milgram's agentic theory, denial, compliance, authoritarian personality, and binding forces of rule and role orientation. Constructive obedience can have survival value.

Further reading

Aronson, E. (1995) *The Social Animal* (7th edition), New York: W. H. Freeman. This book tends to dwell on compliance but Milgram's work is covered. There are a number of excellent sections on ethics and the social psychologist.

Manstead, A. and Hewstone, M. (1995) *The Blackwell Encyclopaedia of Social Psychology*, Oxford: Blackwell. This book, as the name implies, has explanatory sections on compliance, obedience and many of the other key terms used in this chapter. There are further explanations as to how destructive obedience occurs.

Answer the following either verbally or in written note form.

1 Why do people obey?
2 What is the difference between constructive and destructive obedience?
3 How might culture affect the degree to which we are obedient?

Review exercise

2

Conformity

Introduction

Throughout our daily lives we conform, i.e. we behave in response to the perceived pressure of others. We queue, wait at bus stops and conform to road signs. In other situations our **conformity** is subtler. When in a group we often 'go with the flow' while at the same time having some private reservations about what we are doing. In such face-to-face contact with a group we are under pressure to conform to the beliefs, actions and attitudes of the 'greater' group. In this respect our behaviour can be governed by a number of social influences of which obedience and conformity to group influences are examples. We need to be careful here not to confuse behaviour changed as a result of conformity and behaviour changed as a result of obedience. Although definitions differ slightly from psychologist to psychologist the following differences can be observed:

- In conformity situations behaviour changes as a result of group pressure, despite there being no explicit requirement on the part of individual participants to change. In this respect behaviour within the group becomes more homogenous.
- In obedience situations behaviour changes as a result of the explicit instructions of an authority figure, i.e. the experimenter. In this respect behaviour arises out of the fact that social structure is differentiated, i.e. the experimenter begins with a higher status.

(after Evans, 1980)

In this chapter we are going to examine material that deals with behaviour altered as a result of manipulating group pressure, i.e. conformity.

Mustafer Sherif and informational social influences

Study

In a classic study of conformity, Sherif (1935) asked participants to observe a stationary light in a darkened room and report on its movement. They did this first on their own and then in groups. What the participants were actually observing was an optical illusion called the **autokinetic effect**. If you stare at a spot of light in the dark the light appears to move. This happens for two reasons. The eye is never still even when you are staring and the other reason is that the eye has no other reference point. Sherif asked his participants to estimate the amount of movement of the light.

Sherif was testing the idea that people, in conditions of uncertainty, need the behaviour of others to provide information. The estimates were wider, in terms of their range, when participants were alone, than when in groups. Sherif observed that in small groups of two or three estimates converged about the group mean. In the case of some groups they all gave virtually the same estimate. Most importantly this phenomenon persisted after group sessions when participants were tested separately again. Sherif believed that what had happened was that, as the task was difficult, participants had used the group **frame of reference**, i.e. they used the context in which an event takes place and is judged, in order to deal with the task's uncertainty.

Evaluation

One of the problems with this research is that the autokinetic effect is difficult to measure, i.e. we do not know how small or how large the effect is, making it difficult to determine the amount of conformity which took place. General health, age and visual acuity probably influence the autokinetic effect.

Others have criticised the research because it only tells us about one type of conformity. Deutsch and Gerard (1955) point to two alternative explanations of conformity: **normative** and **informational influences**. Deutsch and Gerard theorised that individuals have a need to feel secure about their beliefs, feelings and perceptions of the world. This is probably why so many of us seek advice from our families, friends and lovers about all kinds of things from relationship problems to which car or computer to buy. Informational influences occur when individuals accept information from another in order to make sense out of reality, especially if reality is ambiguous. Psychologists believe that Sherif's study is an illustration of the latter.

Normative influences, on the other hand, occur because as humans we have a need for social acceptance and approval. We often go along with the group because we dislike disapproval, we want to achieve a specific goal and being accepted is thought to be necessary to achieve it or we simply just enjoy cultivating approval in others. The following study is an example of this.

Solomon Asch and normative social influences

Study

Another psychologist called Solomon Asch (1951, 1952, 1956) conducted a series of experiments that were much more tightly controlled than those of Sherif. (See article 2 in the key research summaries in chapter 6. Read this now.) His procedure became the standard for most replications by others investigating variables in conformity such as gender and culture, as we shall see later.

Evaluation

The summaries of Asch's results are misleading though. A closer examination of all of Asch's results shows that despite an overall yield to group pressure, i.e. normative influence, there are many individual differences. Some participants did not conform, conformity was not consistent in all participants, and the range of responses was wide.

These variations are important since they point to the possibility that Asch may have been testing a number of aspects of conformity or a much more complex situation than was first thought, as we will discuss below.

Asch's interviews with his participants after the experiments showed that many of them were clearly anxious. This stemmed partly from their desire to be in harmony with the rest of the group (the confederates of Asch), which meant they had to deny the evidence of their own eyes. They also thought it could be damaging to be a dissenter. Asch reports that many of the non-yielders 'longed' to agree with the majority. One of Asch's strongest non-yielders remarked: 'It is more pleasant if one is in agreement.' Another described his feelings as: 'I felt disturbed, puzzled, separated like an outcast from the rest. Every time I disagreed I was beginning to wonder if I wasn't beginning to look funny.' Like Milgram, this aspect has ethical implications. Was Asch 'right' to misinform his participants and subject them to such feelings?

In Asch's experiments normative influences were at work. The participants were responding to the demands of **social identity**, i.e. the part of the self that comes from being a member of a social group, rather than just participating in a task which required them to make a judgement based on an informational task.

Informational and normative influences

Deutsch and Gerard (1955) carried out a still more controlled experiment with three conditions. All experiments were of the Asch baseline type, e.g. judgement of line length. The three groups were:

- three stooges, all gave incorrect answers and one participant (group pressure);

- participants responded anonymously and in private (no group pressure);
- an accuracy group where group pressure was brought to bear on the group to be as accurate as possible (maximum group pressure).

In addition, half the participants were allowed to respond while the stimuli were present and the other half when the stimuli had been removed. This was in order to manipulate the ambiguity of the situation and therefore the group pressure and the uncertainty of the response. The results showed that decreasing group pressure and uncertainty reduced conformity. The most surprising result was that 23% still conformed when isolated and when uncertainty was low. This demonstrates that group pressure is a factor in the degree of conformity shown but at the same time also shows that both normative and informational forces may be at work. Many psychologists agree that in real-world situations both may work a part and it may be very difficult to separate them. In other words, we may well 'go with the flow' because we wish to be like others in our group but at the same time we may well be looking to others for information.

Answer the following either verbally or in written note form:

1 Briefly describe the experiments of Sherif and Asch.
2 How do they differ in terms of informational and situational explanations?
3 Try to define the difference between conformity and obedience.

Progress exercise

Richard Crutchfield

Crutchfield's study

Asch's published research prompted others to investigate conformity including Crutchfield (1955) who placed participants in separate booths, six at a time with a visual display. Visual discrimination puzzles similar to those used by Asch were projected onto each screen. Questions were asked such as: which has the greater area, a star or a circle? (The circle was about one-third larger in diameter.) Participants responded by pressing a button and each participant's responses were displayed for all of them to see. Participants did not know that the 'other' responses were hypothetical. Crutchfield displayed to each participant answers that seemed to show that the 'others', or a substantial proportion of them, had given a wrong answer, e.g. that a star has a greater surface area than a circle with a larger diameter. This enabled Crutchfield to manipulate group pressure.

Crutchfield carried out his experiment on over 600 participants and like Asch conducted various modifications, i.e. with or without a co-dissenter. Like Asch he also found a high level of conformity. In one experiment involving 50 military personnel, the degree of conformity was as high as 46% (Crutchfield, 1954). Crutchfield took this as evidence that there might be a higher degree of conformity in society than we think. He found also that the more definite the answer, the lower the conformity level, i.e. he distinguished between normative and informational influences.

Evaluation

Crutchfield's findings seem to confirm the research of Asch and Sherif. They show also that participants do not have to be physically present, as in the Asch and Sherif studies, for conformity to occur. In other words, normative influences can be seen to take place when we are under the impression that others (unseen) are aware of our responses. But we must criticise his experiment with military personnel, in so far as military training places great emphasis on both conformity and obedience, i.e. military discipline. The high levels of conformity therefore may have occurred because of their military experiences, rather than because of normative or informational influences, or a combination of both.

Conformity/non-conformity and physiology

In 1961 Bogdonoff *et al.* conducted a similar experiment in which participants were subjected to group pressure influences. While the participants were working at the various perception tasks Bogdonoff and his associates were able to measure **autonomic arousal**, i.e. changes in the autonomic nervous system. This is possible for example by measuring blood pressure before, during and after an experiment to see how the body reacts to a change in our social environment. Generally speaking, if you make a person anxious there is a rise in autonomic functioning, such as blood pressure, as the body tries to cope with the new situation and re-establish equilibrium. In Bogdonoff's experiment the general effect was a change in fatty acid levels in as much as:

- conformers generally showed a decrease in fatty acid levels
- non-conformers generally showed an increase.

It is reasonable to deduce from this study that it confirms the work of Crutchfield in so far as non-conformity may make us anxious whereas conformity may make us feel more comfortable because we feel like everyone else, rather than the odd one out. You may think that this is substantial support for the argument that behaviour is subject to group pressure and in turn this is reflected in bodily functioning but there are problems in assuming that physiological change is always associated in some way with mental change, and vice versa.

One of the problems with this type of research is that like Sherif's it is difficult to get a baseline from which to work, i.e. one person's physiological responses to change may not be typical of the entire group, and similarly an average may not be typical of any one individual. Aspects of physiology such as changes in the blood pressure and galvanic skin response are attractive to social scientists because they can be measured accurately. But the problem comes in matching it to a psychological assessment. What I consider to be very anxiety provoking and place at 8 on a rating scale of 0–10 may show a rather *low* level of physiological change in arousal.

Progress exercise

Answer the following either verbally or in written note form:

1 Summarise the findings of Crutchfield.
2 What does isolation from the group do to the level of conformity?
3 Can you explain your answer for 2?

Factors that may influence the degree of conformity

Both Asch and Crutchfield carried out a number of variations of their basic experiment, e.g. allowing the participant to have a fellow dissenter, putting them near the beginning of the group rather than at the end or by altering the composition of the group, i.e. businessmen rather than undergraduates. The following is a summary of their findings:

- When asked privately, previous yielders often revert back to their private opinion, but not all (Asch).
- The composition and size of a group can influence the degree of conformity, e.g. whether the bogus majority are undergraduates or professionals with a 'perceived' higher social status (Asch and Crutchfield).
- Experiments then and since seem to show that a majority of between 3 and 7 is sufficient to obtain conformity. (See the section on majority size and conformity, p. 31.)
- Yielding is by no means consistent, e.g. some participants become increasingly more yielding and vice versa (Asch and Crutchfield).
- There are large individual differences (Asch).
- Rates of conformity are low when tasks are difficult (Asch and Crutchfield).
- Despite the latter many studies have demonstrated that yielding to group pressure can be achieved in some despite the consensus of the bogus majority being manifestly wrong (Asch and Crutchfield).

- When the participant had a fellow dissenter (really a confederate of the experimenter) conformity to the majority was difficult to achieve (Asch and Crutchfield).
- If a fellow participant (really a confederate of the experimenter) makes a mistake, e.g. says it is line 3 rather than 1, conformity drops (Asch and Crutchfield).
- Non-conformers are present in nearly all studies (Asch and Crutchfield, but see chapter 3 on independent behaviour).
- There are gender and cultural differences in the rate of conformity.
- Personality factors may influence rates of conformity (Crutchfield, see also chapter 3 on independent behaviour).

Majority size and conformity

Asch (1955) conducted baseline experiments where the size of the majority group varied from 1 to 13. He found that conformity was at its optimum when the number of confederates of the experimenter who gave false answers was between 3 and 7. Interestingly after 9 there was a decrease in conformity. It would appear from this and the work of Rosenberg (1961) and Stang (1976) that conformity increases as the majority group size increases to 3. From 3 to 7 maximum conformity is produced. After this the size of the group has little difference on the behaviour of the participants or it produces a slight decrease, about 5–7%.

Wilder (1977) explained this by arguing that when groups are large, participants may be suspicious of their unanimity. He observed also that size needs to be qualified in terms of how many independent sources of influence are brought to bear on the participant. Five confederates perceived as in collusion with each other, for example, would have less effect than three confederates all seen as independent of each other. This seems to show that *how* participants view each other is as important as group size. We will look at this again when we consider independent behaviour.

Answer the following either verbally or in written note form:

1 List four factors a researcher might manipulate to investigate their influence on conformity.
2 What has research shown about the relationship between group size and conformity?

Cultural differences and conformity

Studies

Another aspect of conformity investigated has been the role of culture. The most famous is the research done by Milgram (1961). Using a modified form of the Asch-type group pressure technique Milgram compared the conformity rates of Norwegian and French participants. Each participant had to judge the duration of two tones delivered through earphones. Each participant would hear the responses of five other 'participants' before giving their own. On 16 of the 30 trials the judgements were wrong. Milgram reported conformity in 62% of Norwegian participants and 50% of French participants.

Evaluation

In a second repeat of the experiment participants were told that the results would be used in the design of aircraft safety signals, therefore linking the performance of each participant to a life-or-death situation. On this second trial, conformity rates were lower for both groups but the Norwegians were still scoring higher than the French.

In a third study the participants were allowed to record their responses in private having previously delivered their judgement out loud and been led to believe that five other participants were listening to them. In this series of trials overall conformity dropped considerably but the Norwegian participants conformed the most. In a fourth series of trials, non-conformers were targeted and criticised for not taking the majority view. Conformity increased significantly in both groups, the Norwegians yielded on 75% of trials whereas French participants yielded on 59% of trials. Milgram reports in addition that there were differences in the way that each culture dealt with the criticism. Norwegian non-yielders were much more accepting of the criticism whereas the French were more retaliatory.

Milgram felt that these differences stemmed from the cultural differences between French and Norwegian society. He saw Norwegian society as being 'highly cohesive' and Norwegians as possessing a 'deep feeling of group identification'. He viewed the French as demonstrating 'far less consensus in both social and political life'.

Since Milgram's classic study there have been many comparisons of cultures and conformity. Smith and Bond (1993) compiled thirty-one published studies of conformity using Asch's baseline experiment or an adaptation of it. The overall level of conformity recorded from cultures as diverse as Fijian, African and Western was an average of 31.2% with a range of 44%.

The highest conformity was observed in **collectivist** cultures. These are societies, where one's meaning as a person is expressed through relationships and/or the social group to which one is attached. Similarly, the lowest rates of conformity were recorded in cultures that tolerate *individualism*. This is seen more often in Western countries. Relationships within and between groups are looser. The autonomy of the individual rather than the group they belong to is seen as important. In relation to conformity, collectivist cultures, because they encourage uniformity at the expense of individuality, encourage values and beliefs that make it easier to be a conformist. In cultures where autonomy is encouraged the reverse may be happening in so far as unanimity and conformity may be frowned upon.

Gender and conformity

Studies

Early researchers such as Crutchfield (1955) and Krech *et al.* (1962) hypothesised that women would be more conforming than men on the grounds that male and female **gender roles** were different. The female gender role was characterised by Krech *et al.* as: 'Promulgation of conventional values ... dependence upon the group, submissiveness to males, avoidance of disagreement with others in the interests of group harmony.' The typical male gender role, on the other hand, was defined as laying: 'more stress on the ideals of self-sufficiency, self-assertion, independence of thought'. Reading this now, you may feel they do not reflect current attitudes in society, but you must remember these views were expressed over 35 years ago. At the time there was evidence to support the prediction. In baseline Asch-type experiments and in Crutchfield's replications it was found that:

- Females scored higher on measure of conformity.
- As testing proceeded the differences between male and female scores widened.
- High-conforming females tended to be 'characterised by easier acceptance of the conventional feminine role'.
- Female dissenters were characterised by 'marked signs of conflict in their feelings about the conventional feminine role and lower '**socialisation**' scores on a test of personality.

(Gough, 1960)

Other evidence was marshalled too to support the hypothesis, such as work at the time on 'persuasibility', which was defined as a readiness to accept social influence, irrespective of its form, e.g. personal communication, radio programme or magazine advertisement. Researchers in the field of social influences had found gender differences, in that females were more susceptible to 'persuasibility' than males, confirming the hypothesis that women were seen at the time as submissive whereas men were viewed as assertive.

More recent studies point to the fact that although females conform slightly more than males, the differences are small. In addition, the differences may have more to do with the task and the gender of the experimenter. In other words, the experiments of the 1950s and 1960s were flawed and may well have reflected male/female **gender stereotypes** prevalent at the time. More careful studies (Javornisky, 1979) have revealed that women conform more than men only when:

- the task is male-orientated;
- the experimenter is a male.

Sistrunk and McDavid (1971) exposed male and female groups to group pressure in identifying various stereotypic male and female items, e.g. wrench (male), stitching (female). Mixed groups of participants were exposed to semi-ambiguous items similar to the above, i.e. traditionally associated with masculine or feminine behaviour. They had to identify them as a group. In addition there were neutral items such as a popular singer (non-sex stereotype). Predictably males conformed more on female items, females conformed more on male items, and on neutral items they scored the same.

Evaluation

Role theory could be an explanation for these small differences in gender conformity. This theory proposes that like 'actors' in a social 'drama' our separate roles in society will express various attitudes, beliefs and norms of behaviour. In the 1950s and 1960s, the traditional male/female divide was along the lines of male, dominant worker and female, submissive homemaker. Women in the past and still to an extent today have lower status in society; there are few high-status women such as judges or company directors and more often than men they have part-time, low-paid jobs. As these traditional gender roles disappear from society one may predict that gender differences in conformity will change also.

Answer the following either verbally or in written note form:

1 List some of the situational variations attempted by experimenters to observe their effect on conformity rates.
2 With reference to Milgram's conformity experiments state what they seem to show about culture and conformity.
3 Briefly outline how role theory can explain gender differences and conformity rates.

Progress exercise

Evaluation of conformity experiments

Validity

All of these studies lack ecological validity, i.e. because they were performed under very rigid and controlled conditions and therefore do not represent real-world situations. In real life, if I disagree, I may be seen as a deviant or hero by those around me. My need to be different may be brought home to me by not being admitted to a wine bar because I am wearing jeans. On the other hand I can see how others are rewarded for their conformity because they are not being asked to leave as they are wearing trousers. Rather than send me home to get changed my friends may say: 'Well in that case we will all leave and go somewhere else.' Or, as I saw once, the girl in jeans went to the toilet and emerged in a skirt made out of loo paper!

Social situations are very complex. To replicate this complexity would be very difficult because of all the possible confounding variables that would have to be controlled.

Ethics

Another criticism aimed at these studies is the fact that many of them were unethical. Participants were not fully informed of the nature of the experiment and its consequences. You may feel this is a little harsh as all of the participants were debriefed afterwards. However, you could argue that if this is to be the standard then in theory you could perform any number of potentially harmful experiments as long as you debrief your participants afterwards.

Aronson (1995) makes the point that experimental social psychologists must weigh the benefits of research to society against the responsibility to the individual participant. It is clearly very important after deceiving a participant and subjecting him or her to an intense experience to return the participant to society in the same frame of mind as she or he entered the laboratory. Many experiments clearly have benefit to all, in that they may help us explain important issues such as racism. As Aronson emphasises, the greater the issue under investigation the greater the benefit to society. You could argue therefore that such studies are worth the possible damage they may do to both the participant and the reputation of psychology.

Historical context

Many psychologists point also to the fact that the experiments may well be a product of the historical period and situations they were conducted in, e.g. a post-war American university campus. Perrin and Spencer (1980), using British students, repeated Asch's conformity experiments and did not find as much conformity as the earlier experiments, e.g. out of 396 responses, only one participant conformed. This indicates, perhaps, that as society changed, in this case from a post-war economy recovering from the privations of the World War II, conformity rates changed. In Perrin and Spencer's study, nearly 30 years later, British university students were from a different set of socio-economic circumstances. However, in order to obtain 'naïve' participants they used science and engineering students. Science and engineering graduates may be much more concerned with accurate measurement because of their training and therefore are less easily swayed.

Doms and Avermaet (1981) conducted similar research using participants from less mathematical disciplines and were able to confirm Asch's original results – i.e. their participants conformed on about 35% of trials.

As we mentioned earlier in the section on culture there have been many studies since Asch's original in many cultures, and nearly all of them have found a degree of conformity (Smith and Bond, 1993). Could it be that Perrin and Spencer's results are odd or is it that the state we have so far been referring to as conformity has other dimensions?

Answer the following either verbally or in written note form:

1   Why are the experiments of Asch and Crutchfield criticised for not having ecological validity?
2   Describe the ethical issues involved in performing conformity studies of the type used by Asch and Crutchfield.

Progress exercise

Explaining the conformity effect

Compliance

Perrin and Spencer (1980) noted that Asch debriefed his participants and reported that many had conformed in the experiment but did not believe that the others were necessarily correct. He pointed to the likelihood that a dual situation existed, in that:

- Participants outwardly agreed with the group; they behaved in an expedient manner.
- Inwardly they disagreed.

He called this **compliance**; i.e. individuals agree with the majority but do not alter their private beliefs. Many of us have done this, for example, not wanting to be the odd one out, we go with our friends to the 'Pig and Hook' knowing full well that one person has been told we will be at the 'Pheasant'. We know that our behaviour is unkind, even wrong, but because we want to appear to be a 'team player' we go along with the rest. Conformity at this level then is transitory and is only observable so long as the 'team' is physically around.

Identification

Kelman postulated further that some individuals both inwardly and outwardly agree with the group, therefore changing their fundamental attitude: they identify with the group. He called this **identification**. Many of us have witnessed this either in ourselves, in family members or friends. The classic case is the boy or girl meets partner situation. As the relationship deepens they appear to change; e.g. the boy takes up gardening and DIY, which are interests of his girlfriend.

An alternative explanation of identification comes from psychoanalysis. Freud believed that in anxiety-provoking situations many of us resort to defence mechanisms, i.e. an automatic response, to deal with the situation. In the case of group pressure it could be that we are really using identification to deal with the fact that we do not wish to appear as the odd one out. We identify with the group, rather than cope with the feelings of inadequacy and doubt, which accompany being independent. This is very similar to Kelman's explanation but there are fundamental differences in that for Freud identification results from anxiety and the identification behaviour is automatic in that it is triggered by the stress of the situation. Kelman saw it as a fundamental change in attitude, i.e. an enduring organisation of beliefs, feelings and behavioural tendencies. Because the person is seen to behave in a way contrary to their beliefs, e.g. contradict the evidence from their own eyes, they are conforming because they are identifying with the group norm. In other words they have experienced a major attitude change.

Answer the following either verbally or in written note form:

1 With the help of the glossary try to define the difference between conformity and compliance.
2 Briefly describe the Freudian idea of identification as an explanation for conformity.

Progress exercise

Summary

Sherif noted convergence in group averages when participants estimated in groups. Asch and Crutchfield demonstrated that majority group influence could have a powerful effect on minorities. Examination of all results does show a wide variation and qualitative differences, e.g. increasing or decreasing conformity from one trial to another. Replication studies seem to confirm Asch's and Crutchfield's original findings. But this is not universally true – quantitative differences have been noted between some cultures, genders and group sizes. The original studies have been criticised on the grounds of ethics and ecological validity and on re-examination the concept of conformity has been questioned. Deutsch and Gerard offered an alternative explanation based on normative and informational influences. Other explanations of conformity include the psychodynamic concept of identification.

Try and match the correct researcher(s) with the correct concept/item/method/ etc. Not all items in the right-hand column can be matched.

	autonomic arousal
	ethics
Asch (1952)	Freudian
Doms and Avermaet (1981)	cultural influences
Crutchfield (1955)	replication study which confirms Asch's results
Smith and Bond (1993)	normative and informational influences
Deutsch and Gerard (1955)	studies on children
Sherif (1935)	group size
Milgram (1961)	autokinetic effect
Shanab and Yahya (1977)	military personnel
Perrin and Spencer (1980)	identification
	ecological validity
	collectivist cultures

Further reading

Deaux, K., Dane, F. and Wrightsman, L. (1993) *Social Psychology in the '90s*, 6th edition, Pacific Grove, CA: Brooks/Cole. This book has a long chapter on social influences much of which is concerned with conformity and compliance. It goes into much more detail on the differences between conformity and compliance than I have been able to do here.

Lord, C. (1997) *Social Psychology*, Harcourt Brace College Publishers. This is a weighty tome, well illustrated and colourful. It tends to take the view that majority and minority influences can be interpreted through normative and informational influences.

3

Independent
behaviour

Introduction

The last chapter focused on conformity, but history is littered with individuals, such as Jesus Christ or Galileo, who took an independent view against the tide of popular opinion.

In this chapter we are going to examine behaviour which can be described as independent. I am going to do this by looking at aspects of both conformity and obedience that tend to decrease conformity or obedience and therefore by implication increase independent behaviour or anti-conformity.

There are at least three ways of explaining why people do not conform to group norms: **anti-** or counter-**conformity**, independent behaviour, and disobedience.

Counter-conformity and independent behaviour

Study

Schien (1957) reported the results of interviews with US prisoners of war involved in the Korean War of 1950–53. The psychologists were specifically interested in why some of them did not collaborate with their captors, e.g. by agreeing to be filmed criticising the American involvement in the war. They identified two types of resisters:

- Soldiers who knew that admitting guilt for the war was wrong (independent resisters).
- Soldiers who had a long history, both in the US forces and as prisoners of war, of unwillingness to accept authority (counter-conformists).

Evaluation

Schien's study is based on case studies, which while having a greater degree of ecological validity than say a laboratory role-play, often suffer from participant/interviewer bias. Retelling stressful experiences to a researcher may be a very subjective experience from the point of view of the participant. It may be very difficult to separate fact from fiction brought on by the psychological damage these POWs may have suffered as a result of their stressful experience.

Putting this to one side it does seem to show that there may be a qualitative difference between a person who acts independently of a group and a person who is an anti-conformist. **Independent behaviour** can be defined, therefore, as behaviour that does not respond to group norms. If I express my individuality by continuing to do without a telephone, radio, television and video, when nearly everyone else has these things, I may be demonstrating independence. If, on the other hand, I throw out all my worldly goods because I want to be different and not like everyone else, I may be demonstrating **counter-conformity**. In the case of the latter, I am in opposition to the norms of the group rather than not responding to them as in the former case. Aronson (1995) points out that in relation to conformity, those who conform are often seen as team players, i.e. seen positively, whereas those who are independent or non-conformist are seen as deviant, i.e. seen negatively.

On the other hand, we often idolise those who have been 'deviant'. We call them freedom fighters or prophets or great leaders. Evans (1980) in a discussion with another famous social psychologist, Darley, points out that some non-comformists are often 'wedded' to a culture of deviance, i.e. some individuals conform to their social group's definition of being different, which is not really being independent. As an example, Darley points to the hippy movement of the 1960s. Young people, in particular, rejected traditional modes of dress, appearance and life-style. What began as an anti-establishment movement soon developed a deviant culture to which its members were all expected to conform. Darley added to this that members of cults often develop a view of themselves as an **ingroup** surrounded by a hostile majority. For their own survival, therefore, they encourage conformity.

Independent behaviour and conformity studies

Asch, like Crutchfield, was aware of the fact that some participants were consistent non-conformers, albeit a few. And, as I pointed out in the previous chapter both Asch and others varied the parameters of their original experiments and found that gender, culture and majority size could affect the degree of conformity and thus the degree of independence. Asch, therefore, experimented with a number of variations to examine the relationship between independence and conformity.

Study: minority of one

Asch (1951) examined this phenomenon by conducting a study, using the length of line task, in which one participant (confederate) amongst 16 true participants gave incorrect answers. The majority, confident and self-assured, treated the confederates' answers with disbelief and ridicule.

Evaluation

This seems to show that an independent participant can have a profound effect; even if it is only for the majority to laugh at them because they perceive them as 'beyond the fringe' non-conformists or individualists. In addition, it seems to show that a group will use punishment to make the deviate fall into line.

In relation to the latter point, Schachter (1951), using the Asch design, had groups of participants read and discuss the case study of a juvenile delinquent. Each group consisted of approximately 5 to 7 participants. Into each group he introduced an additional, paid confederate. Their brief was to establish themselves in the following roles:

- Deviate: a group member who took a view that was in opposition to the general opinion of the group, i.e. behaved independently of them.
- Modal: a group member who took a view that conformed to the average of the real participants.
- Slider: a group member who initially had a view similar to the deviate but who changed to the view of the modal participant.

In nearly all the experiments, more communication was directed at the deviate than the other two. In highly cohesive groups, the communication towards the deviate rose to a peak then fell away to the point where the deviate was virtually ignored. Little attention was paid to the modal participant since he conformed. The slider drew much attention until he conformed and then communication towards him fell away. This seems to confirm in part the Asch study in so far as rather than ridicule the deviate, the groups choose to persuade and, when this did not work (as in the case of the deviate), they ostracised (punished) the deviates. We can conclude from these studies that individual independence or counter-conformity comes at a price. For my personal independence or counter-conformity I may lose the support of my fellows or may have to suffer their ridicule or criticism.

Minorities do not seem to suffer the same extreme censure. Asch was interested too in what would happen to rates of conformity when minorities of two or more were confronted with a unanimous majority.

Study: independent participant with a partner

Asch conducted one series of experiments, using the length of line paradigm, where he allowed the true participant a partner (although the participant was not informed of this prior to the experiment). The confederates would give their incorrect responses but amongst them would be a lone dissenter, who would give a correct response. When it came to the turn of the true participant to give his response he was more likely to disagree with the majority. In most cases the degree of conformity dropped considerably amongst the true participants from 33% to 5%. Even when the supporter deserted the true participant halfway through the series of tasks, the effect was still present in the true participant's responses.

Evaluation

Allowing the true participant a co-dissenter achieves two things:

- It stops the true participant from appearing to be deviate, i.e. non-conforming, within a unanimous majority.
- It allows the participant to be a member of a unanimous sub-group, i.e. the true participant and the other dissenter.

Because the majority was presented with a unanimous sub-group, it would appear to have affected the true participant in so far as it encouraged him to take an independent stance, even when the partner rejoined the majority.

Study: minority v. majority

In another variation of his baseline study, Asch used 11 true/correct participants against 9 deviant/incorrect participants. The general atmosphere was not one of mockery (as had occurred when he used a single confederate with a group of participants) but of seriousness.

Evaluation

This seems to show that the minority had had some influence over the majority, albeit not to change their mind about the length of line. This seems to demonstrate that the minority was viewed as an independent group with a view, rather than as deviates or non-conformists to be censured or ridiculed.

Ambiguity of task

In addition to the above Asch conducted other variations such as making the task obvious or ambiguous. Ambiguity was achieved by making the differences between the lines so slight it was difficult to be sure. In the case of ambiguous tasks, participants were much more likely to behave independently of the group.

Conclusion

Like conformity, independent behaviour and counter-conformity are likely to be influenced by both normative and informational factors. In relation to the above then, and taking into consideration many other variations of Asch's baseline experiment, it would seem that independent behaviour is increased if:

- situations are ambiguous
- the power of the majority is decreased
- the participant is placed near the beginning rather than the end of a group of confederates, thereby reducing the influence of the majority
- participants are allowed to give their answers anonymously or privately
- the participant feels he or she is a member of a divided rather than a cohesive group.

Personality factors in conformity and independence

Crutchfield

As well as conducting studies in conformity Crutchfield collected other data on all of his participants, e.g. he gave them a personality questionnaire and IQ test. In this way he was able to look for differences between conformers and non-conformers, e.g. such as whether conformers or non-conformers in his experiments were rated as more or less anxious. Others, using the Crutchfield paradigm, such as Gough (1960) examined the relationship between conformity/independence and self-perception. Nadler (1959) examined the F-scale ratings of both conformers and independents. Gough and Nadler found differences between conformers and individuals who were more independent of the group. In terms of independence v. conformity the following findings are typical (Krech *et al.*, 1962):

Trait	Conformers	Independents
Cognitive functioning	less intelligent	more intelligent
Motivation/emotion	more anxious	less anxious
Self-concept	lack self-confidence/less insightful	realistic self-perception
Interpersonal relations	poor judgement of others	more self-contained and autonomous
Attitudes/values	conventional/moralistic	more original

These findings support the general view within this interpretation that conformers are low in self-esteem, IQ and status and are high in anxiety and insecurity. Independents, on the other hand, are more intelligent, less anxious and do not need the social approval of a group to the same degree as conformers. Krech's findings seem to show that conformers may well be more dependent on informational and normative influences than their independent counter-parts, who because of their superior intelligence and realistic outlook may be able to resist more successfully the implicit and explicit social pressure of group influences.

Evaluation

We must bear in mind that much of this research is based on correlation studies, which have inherent flaws. Correlation studies only show a relationship and are not controlled experiments. In the case of some negative or positive correlations between conformity/independence and an aspect of personality, the correlation has been as low as 0.3–0.4 indicating a relationship of only 9% to 16%. Some psychologists would say that this is hardly significant and may have occurred by chance.

Evidence that individuals (whether conformers or independents) are not consistent in their conformity or independence throws some doubt onto the hypothesis that personality factors are the sole explanation as to why some are more independent than others (Barron, 1953). Situational factors such as the task in hand or the status of the group we are with may be just as important in determining the degree of independence or conformity shown in addition to aspects of our personality.

Progress exercise

Answer the following either verbally or in written note form:

1 Describe the difference between independence and anticonformity.
2 List and describe three aspects of personality and conformity and independence.

Independent behaviour and obedience studies

Both the anecdotal and experimental evidence leave us with few conclusions other than the fact that within any social collective some have the power to command respect for authority and to impose moral and social behaviour. Obedience is a powerful social influence, so why do people disobey?

Rebellion and obedience

Case studies

Some of Milgram's participants refused to continue with the study when they thought that the 'learner' was in distress, i.e. they rebelled. Gretchen Brandt is an example. Gretchen refused to continue after reaching 210 volts. Milgram (1974) reports that she calmly refused to comply and that, on being questioned as to why, she replied that she had grown up in Nazi Germany and felt that she had witnessed too much pain. Milgram explained this by saying that the experiment had triggered Gretchen's painful memories of her past which in turn had 'awakened' her from her agentic state. Now, in her autonomous state she felt responsible for her actions and therefore refused to continue to obey the instructions of the experimenter.

Disobedient role models

In one variation of the standard procedure, Milgram (1974) intro-duced two additional confederates as teachers. The standard procedure in this experiment was as follows:

- Teacher 1 (confederate) read the list of words.
- Teacher 2 (confederate) told the learner (confederate) whether he was correct or not.
- Teacher 3 (participant) would administer the shock.

All obeyed the experimenter's instructions till the 150 volt shock when Teacher 1 refused to continue but remained in the room taking no further part in the study. After the 210 volt shock Teacher 2 also refused to continue and the experimenter instructed the participant to continue alone. Only 10% of participants continued to complete the full series.

An interesting variation conducted by Rosenhan (1969) using confederates also illustrates the power of disobedient role models over others. Rosenhan had four conditions:

1 A replication of Milgram's baseline condition (control).
2 A condition in which the participant saw the model (confederate) protest but still gave the maximum shock.
3 A condition in which the model (confederate) stormed out of the room on discovering that the experimenter was an unsupervised undergraduate.
4 A condition in which the model (confederate) informed the experimenter that he could not continue, because the learner was in great pain.

In the first situation the participant's obedience rates were reduced as much as in the third case where the confederate stormed out, demon-strating the influence of a disobedient role model, whether the reason for the disobedience was legitimate (concern for the welfare of the learner) or incidental (dispute over the experimenter's qualifications). It would appear that seeing a disobedient role model might be more important than knowing the reason for their disobedience.

Both of these studies seem to demonstrate that disobedient role models can limit the effectiveness of a malevolent authority figure in so far as their disobedience may encourage independent behaviour or rebellion in others. Research into altruism demonstrates also the power of positive and constructive role models on helping behaviour. Participants who observe role models being altruistic or helpful often show this influence in their own behaviour after being exposed to a real or filmed model.

Independence as a group norm

Others disagree, Gamson *et al.* (1982) pointed to the fact that what may be taking place is a choice between obedience and conformity to group norms. (See article 3 of the key research summaries in chapter 6 for a detailed description of Gamson's experiment. Read this now.)

Gamson points out that as the situation developed, i.e. one or more role model(s) disobeyed the co-ordinator, resulting in the development of a group norm: a choice between disobedience and conformity to group values. In other words independent behaviour is often conformity to a different set of norms, if they become available.

Evaluation of independence and obedience studies

On the basis of the above then we can say that obedience and conformity are 'potent social forces' which enable some to commit war crimes and encourage others to great acts of bravery. Obedience has survival value in so far as it can contribute to our safety. Rebellion and independent behaviour, on the other hand, seem to occur for three reasons:

- past experience (Gretchen's war-time experiences);
- the social power of role models to limit behaviour (Milgram and Rosenhan);
- conformity to group norms (Gamson)

If we look closely at this evidence though it is quite poor. Disobedient participants in Milgram's studies are few in number and therefore constitute little more than case study evidence; the latter is often biased and not representative of the whole group. The use of role models has been criticised because the experiments are often laboratory studies and therefore lack ecological validity. In addition, many point to the fact that experiments using role models do not always take account of other social influences such as gender differences in behaviour. One of the most frequently observed differences in experiments using role models is that despite similar exposure to an aggressive model, boys demonstrate more aggressive behaviour than girls do, in the post-exposure period. Finally, much of the evidence for independent behaviour is non-experimental and therefore cannot claim to show cause and effect.

A theoretical explanation of independent behaviour: social impact theory

Is it possible then, despite the complexity of group influences, that a single theory can explain them all? If we consider groups in terms of power then we can look at that power in terms of numbers. On a simple level of explanation: the more numerous the more powerful and conversely the less numerous the less powerful. To some extent this can explain conformity studies in so far as the largeness of the majority swayed the true participant into going along with them. But as we have seen in Asch's studies, an individual with a partner, i.e. a minority of two can resist a majority.

Latané and Wolf (1981) drew on social impact theory to try and explain social influences such as independent behaviour, and minority and majority influence. Social impact theory is a **meta-theory**, which claims that social influence will be proportional to a multiplication of strength, immediacy and number of individuals who are the source of the influence and will be inversely proportional to the strength, immediacy and number of individuals being influenced. Applied to independent behaviour, and social influence, therefore, the effect will be dependent on a combination of:

- strength, i.e. perceived power;
- immediacy, i.e. proximity, such as giving your response in private rather than in a group;
- numbers, i.e. an expert might have just as much effect, or more, than a large group of amateurs.

Non-conformists can have a profound effect on a majority even if it is only for the majority to laugh at them or to argue against them because they perceive them as deviates. So, with large majorities, their largeness makes them powerful, but as we saw with the study where a majority was confronted with a large minority with an equally valid message, the majority considered their opinion rather than ridiculed them. Similarly with the ambiguous task, the ambiguity makes everyone an expert witness and, therefore, individuals do not seem to mind being the odd one out and acting independently.

Evaluation

Social impact theory is often described as a 'static' theory, i.e. it is limited to explaining how one individual is affected by their social environment (Manstead and Hewstone,1995). In this respect it is limited in so far as it is difficult to explain groups of individuals acting within or upon other groups or individuals. Others have pointed to the fact that it is mechanistic, like physics it tries to draw on basic laws and principles. The advantage of this is that it is quantifiable and therefore can be subjected to experimentation and mathematical analysis. As pointed out elsewhere, laboratory-based experiments often lack the realism of real-world situations, such as a works meeting or a militarised zone. Some social psychologists feel that the relationship between the individual, the groups s/he belongs to and their interaction with each other is far too complex to be modelled on a few basic laws or principles.

Summary

Independent behaviour is behaviour that does not respond to group norms. Counter-conformity is behaviour that does not correspond with accepted or agreed group norms. Asch and Crutchfield did some research and noted that ambiguity of task, a dissenting partner and personality traits influenced the degree of independence. Social impact theory seems to be able to explain independent behaviour. Independent behaviour within obedience studies points to a number of explanations: past experience, disobedient role models and norm theory.

Review exercise

Describe an occasion when independence was shown. The occasion can be from your own life, a play or film or an occasion you observed or heard about. Try and analyse the occasion in terms of what led up to it, what happened and what were the consequences of the behaviour. Can you detect any elements of what you have learned in this chapter in the incident you have described?

Further reading

Deaux, K., Dane, F. and Wrightsman, L. (1993) *Social Psychology in the '90s*, 6th edition, Brooks/Cole. This book has some more information on this aspect of conformity and anti-conformity.

4

Collective behaviour

Definitions

The term **crowd behaviour**, sometimes referred to as collective behaviour in other textbooks, needs to be defined. Surprisingly, in deciding what constitutes a human crowd, social scientists are fairly clear. Definitions vary, but there is a fair degree of similarity:

Any relatively sizeable collection of people who are in direct interaction with one another in a public place.

(Giddens, 1989)

Behaviour of people en masse, such as in a crowd, protest or riot.

(Hogg and Vaughan, 1995)

A large but temporary gathering of people with a common interest or focus.

(Reber, 1985)

Behaviour in which large numbers of people who are in the same place at the same time behave in a uniform manner which is volatile, appears relatively unorganised, is characterised by strong emotion, and is often in violation of social norms.

(Manstead and Hewstone, 1995)

Along with the above, some social psychologists believe this area of study should include: semi-religious cult gatherings and social movements such as the Moonies; fads and fashions which occasionally sweep a nation such as the punk phenomena of the 1980s; political demonstrations and rallies; rumour transmission such as the lynch mobs of the southern states of the USA in the 1920s and 1930s; and panicking crowds such as at random shootings. An example of the extreme consequence of a human crowd out of control would be that of the Liverpool crowd at Sheffield Wednesday's Hillsborough Stadium in 1989 when scores of fans were either killed or badly injured. But all large gatherings do not end in disaster.

Angry and peaceful crowds

Mann (1981) analysed newspaper reports of crowds present at attempted suicides. One such report was about a Puerto Rican man who attempted to jump from the tenth floor of a building. The crowd below him consisting of approximately 500 was shouting in both Spanish and English to 'Brinca (jump)'. In 10 of the 21 cases of threatened suicide Mann studied, members of the crowd provoked the victim.

Individuals who attempt suicide are often ill or extremely distraught, usually because of depression or a sudden traumatic event. They deserve our pity and patience rather than derision. So why do crowds bait? Mann discovered that in the case of the baiting crowds two factors were very relevant:

- Baiting was more likely to occur if the suicide attempt was in the evening, e.g. after six o'clock.

- By-standers who were close to the victim did not bait, neither did they bait if the victim was above the twelfth floor.

Mann hypothesised, therefore, that proximity and failing light increased hostility. We have already seen in the chapters on obedience and conformity that proximity can influence how we behave. In the case of a crowd, it may well be that darkness and distance play a part in the development of strong emotions. In combination, they bring about a certain amount of anonymity, i.e. loss of identity, while at the same time enhancing arousal. This then increases the likelihood of strong emotions such as aggression.

In opposition to the idea that human collective behaviour is base and aggressive is the work of Durkheim (1893). He was an early observer of social phenomena, but pointed out that peaceful, as opposed to disorderly crowds, served a very good social function in that they tended to contribute to **social cohesion**. Benewick and Holton (1987) interviewed members of the crowd that came to the Wembley Stadium in London in order to attend an open-air mass presided over by Pope Paul. Benewick and Holton found that many of their participants saw the event as powerful and meaningful and the reason they felt this way was because of the sensation of sharing the same feelings with many others. As a case study it certainly seems to support Durkheim's thesis, i.e. crowds can appear to be unanimous in a peaceful activity as well as in anger.

Answer the following either verbally or in written note form:

1 Give one definition of the term 'crowd'.
2 What is the difference between a mob and a peaceful crowd?
3 What two situational factors were noted as important in the baiting crowds studied by Mann?

Progress exercise

Two early theorists

Le Bon

One of the earliest theorists was Le Bon who dwelt on the devastation caused by the French Revolution of 1848. He was both appalled and fascinated by the 'base' and 'primitive' behaviour of mob violence describing it as 'ancestral savagery'. Le Bon identified three aspects he thought contributed to the primitive and homogenous behaviour of a rioting crowd:

- Individuals are anonymous and therefore lose personal responsibility for their actions.
- Sentiments, e.g. aggression, are spread rapidly as a result of contagion (the expression of anger by one individual in a crowd quickly and instinctively transmits to others evoking the same emotion).
- Unconscious, anti-social sentiments are released as a result of suggestion, a process closely analogous to hypnosis.

Gabriel Tarde

Le Bon's theory was developed further by Gabriel Tarde (1903, 1910). His theory is descriptive but more general than Le Bon's and can be applied to both artificial and organised crowds, i.e. 'masses'. Tarde's theory can be used to explain institutional crowds such as soldiers and school pupils as well as 'mob' violence. Tarde saw masses as the underlying force and guiding principle behind the evolution of a society. He too saw the hypnotic and charismatic effect on a crowd of a leader as an important factor in this. But unlike Le Bon, who only saw negativity in collective actions, Tarde theorised that a crowd could be creative as well as destructive. This is possible through suggestibility, i.e. imitation. He considered imitation as the cornerstone of social order. It is through imitation that leaders are able to influence the 'group think' of the masses.

Evaluation of Le Bon and Tarde

Modern social psychologists criticise Le Bon and Tarde as unscientific. They were social theorists who concerned themselves more with the descriptive aspects of behaviour rather than the analytic. Le Bon's work in particular is still held in some regard in so far as it was he who drew our attention to the pathological and abnormal aspects of crowd behaviour.

Answer the following either verbally or in written note form:

1 Write three or four keywords or phrases for each of the theories of Le Bon and Tarde.
2 Note the three aspects observed by Le Bon that he considered contributed to the primitive and homogenous behaviour of a rioting crowd.

Progress exercise

Rule-governed mob behaviour

Another way to explain the behaviour of crowds is to think about how the behaviour might be predictable and governed by rules.

Football crowds

Some evidence from others, e.g. Marsh *et al.* (1978), seems to show that the explosive, spontaneous nature of violent rioting crowds is not wholly to do with frustration or baseness. Marsh studied football crowds, many of which had a tradition amongst the fans of riotous behaviour. Some blamed right-wing elements trying to cause destabilisation. Others blamed the availability of alcohol and yet others saw this as a symptom of a sick society, i.e. because society was dysfunctional large gatherings of youths would easily succumb to rioting. By both observing fans on the terraces and interviewing them, Marsh found a much more complex situation. Far from acting spontaneously, fans operated according to clearly defined rules. Aggression seen on the terraces and after matches was often ritualised. Fans were hurt but this was seen as a breach of the rules. It was more important to show aggression, to 'see off' the other fans by, for example, following them to the railway station, posturing aggressively and using violent language rather than engaging in full-scale rioting.

Marsh found also a clear social structure amongst fans, i.e. junior fans would move 'up' to more prestigious groups of fans because they had shown themselves to be good at the aggression rituals.

Violent incidents did occur and still do. The tragedy at Hillsborough is an example. Marsh believed that occurrences of uncontrolled 'real' violence at stadia could be attributed to unusual or particular individuals, e.g. over-reaction by external agencies or fans, resulting in the breakdown of the rules governing the aggression.

Political rallies

Political rallies have long been associated with instability. Most political rallies are peaceful but occasionally they result in violence often between the demonstrators and the police. Many social psychologists believe that to view such violent behaviour as 'mob' violence or solely as a product of inhuman baseness is too simplistic. Smelser (1962) argues that disorderly crowds happen as a result of the presence of specific social conditions:

- general social tension, e.g. social inequality;
- the presence of agitators, i.e. people who will take direct action;
- a flash point, such as a baton charge by police or stone-throwing agitators;
- a perceived grievance, e.g. the acquittal of four white policemen accused of beating a black motorist, Rodney King, in 1992 in Los Angeles.

Waddington *et al.* (1987) took a similar view. They studied two public rallies which took place during the 12-month long miners' dispute with the then Tory government. The researchers collected data through participant observation, both before and during the events, and through interviews with demonstrators. The first rally was disorderly and violent. The second rally, which took place in the same town two weeks later, was peaceful. Waddington *et al.* maintained that to analyse such incidents on the basis of a flash-point incident or using the concept of mob behaviour was too rudimentary, maintaining that flash points were merely one aspect of very complex social phenomena. Waddington proposed a six-point theoretical model that could be used to analyse this type of social disorder. Although the list appears to be hierarchical Waddington warned against this and argued that all points are important in explaining the 'cause':

Level 1: structural   Wider social structures which govern aspects of whole groups of individuals, such as workers in industries that are on the verge of being restructured, or having their trade-union rights curtailed.

Level 2: political/ideology   A sector of society may have an ideological or political grievance, e.g. freedom to take industrial action in the face of greedy employers. Government legislation may have tightened so much that individuals feel oppressed.

Level 3: cultural   This is about shared ideals and ideas within groups. Ideas about human rights, the need to act, how serious the problem is will all influence the crowd's reactions.

Level 4: contextual   The context in which the demonstration or collective action takes place will be influential also. This will include, for example, the sequence of events leading up to the riot.

Level 5: spatial   This includes the environment in which the event takes place, e.g. urban as opposed to rural areas or whether the area has symbolic significance. Urban areas often provide rioters with unlimited missiles.

Level 6: interactional   This refers to the interaction between the various groups of individuals present at the event, e.g. police, demonstrators, marshals or union officials. Heavy-handed policing may be viewed by the crowd as unjustified, sparking off violent retaliation.

Using the above model Waddington analysed the two miners' rallies. In terms of levels 1, 2 and 3 the rallies were the same, i.e. they both concerned the nature and progress of the protracted miners' strike. In terms of context, situation and interaction the two rallies were very different. In the second, peaceful rally, the setting had been organised carefully, with barriers, entertainment and speakers in order to channel ill-feeling within the crowd into something positive. In addition, the organisers had taken the responsibility for marshalling the crowd upon themselves, therefore allowing the police to keep a discreet distance from the crowd. Many miners viewed the police at the time as agents of the Thatcher government. Thatcher was accused by high-profile union leaders of establishing a police state and, as a result, relations between the miners and the police deteriorated. In the first rally there had been a heavy and immediate police presence. Most officers were dressed in riot gear, suggesting they were expecting a riot anyway. All in all, the second rally passed off without major incident.

Progress exercise

Answer the following either verbally or in written note form:

1 Using Marsh's ideas, can you explain other forms of group violence such as sometimes occurs at fox hunting meetings between the hunters and the hunt saboteurs?

2 List three aspects of human collective behaviour put forward by Smelser as contributing to urban unrest.

3 Using Smelser's ideas explain recent urban unrest associated with the presence of previously convicted paedophiles in local communities.

4 Describe in detail two of Waddington's levels.

Deindividuation

A more empirical approach to explaining collective behaviour is one suggested by Festinger *et al.* (1952) and developed by Zimbardo (1970). Festinger took Jung's (1946) idea of **individuation**, i.e. the process whereby we become progressively more aware of our unique individuality (and all its various parts). The process of deindividuation is almost the reverse of the latter in that on our own we restrict and refrain from what Le Bon would have called 'base' or 'uncivilised' behaviour because we have assimilated strong moral and societal values. In a crowd, these restraints no longer operate and we become deindividuated. Zimbardo postulated that being in a crowd provides individuals with anonymity (as we observed in the baiting crowds at a threatened suicide). This in turn diffuses responsibility for one's own actions, no matter how base, and in turn leads to a loss of identity and reduces our ability to be rational law-abiding individuals. As a result, our behaviour becomes impulsive, as can be seen in a rioting crowd or the outpouring of grief at large funerals.

Research into this phenomenon has tended to investigate the area of anonymity, i.e. the loss of identity contributing to deindividuation. Situational factors such as uniforms, darkness and being a member of a crowd afford us a cloak of anonymity which in turn affects our personal responsibility for the consequence of our actions. Festinger *et al.* (1952) discovered that, when they deindividuated the participants by placing them in a dimly lit room and dressing them in laboratory coats for a group discussion of their parents, they were much more negative about their parents than a similar group in a control condition.

Similar studies, which have used anonymity as the independent variable, have found that physical and verbal aggression increase when participants are deindividuated. The most famous of these is Zimbardo's (1973) Stanford Prison study. (See article 4 of the key research summaries in chapter 6.) In another study by Zimbardo (1970) groups of female students had to give electric shocks to others who made errors in a learning exercise. One group was individuated; e.g. they had nametags, were introduced to each other by name and wore their own clothes. The other group were deindividuated in so far as they had to wear bulky lab coats and hoods (many have commented on the resemblance these clothes had to uniforms worn by the Ku Klux Klan, an extreme, right-wing and racist organisation) and were never referred to individually but as a group. The deindividuated group delivered twice the intensity of shock to the learners as the individuated group.

Diener *et al.* (1976) conducted a naturalistic experiment that took advantage of the festivities associated with Halloween. In many states of America it is traditional for children to dress up as witches, wizards and other such scary characters and go out in the evening of 31 October trick-or-treating (a tradition common in the UK now). The researchers observed the behaviour of 1,352 children (either in small groups or on their own) in 27 targeted homes. Children were greeted by adults at the door of each house and were asked to 'take one of the candies' laid out on a table. Some of them were asked their name (individuated) or they were treated anonymously (deindividuated). The results showed that anonymous, lone children and groups (anonymous or individuated) were more likely to take more than one candy. The transgression rate varied but deindividuated groups stole the most.

Evaluation

Although deindividuation appears to increase the incidence of aggression, theft and insensitivity to the needs of others, replication and part-replication studies have not confirmed that this is so. For example, a part-replication of Zimbardo's prisoner–guard study by Lovibond *et al.* (1979) in Australia also had to be stopped well before the end of the time period for similar reasons, e.g. guards being cruel. Lovibond had changed the situation though in that he dispensed with uniforms and gave 'prisoners' a more humane environment. In this respect, the 'prisoners' were not deindividuated and as such it is an important variation. The fact that the study had to be stopped for similar reasons to Zimbardo's shows that anonymity may play a part in situations such as these. However, other factors, such as role expectation, may be equally important, i.e. Lovibond's participants may well have been performing to the expectations we all have regarding prisoner–gaoler relations.

A study which was a part-replication of Zimbardo's Ku Klux Klan-study adds weight to this conclusion. Johnson and Dowling (1979) repeated the study using three groups:

- One group wore the baggy Ku Klux Klan-type hoods and coat (deindividuated).
- A second group wore nurses' uniforms (deindividuated).
- The third group of women wore either nurses' uniform or the baggy coat and hood but in addition a large name badge (individuated).

The experimenters found that deindividuated, Ku Klux Klan-dressed participants were almost as aggressive as their individuated matches were. Those dressed as nurses were significantly less aggressive than the latter, whether individuated or deindividuated, although the individuated nurses were the least aggressive.

This study seems to show that anti-social behaviour is not necessarily an inevitable consequence of deindividuation and that **role** and **normative expectations**, i.e. what we come to expect to see or experience in a given situation, may be factors in what previous researchers had assumed was deindividuation.

An alternative interpretation

We can explain apparent anti-social behaviour in another way by examining it in terms of private and public self-awareness (Prentice-Dunn and Rogers, 1982; Carver and Scheier, 1981). Rather than concentrate on anonymity, psychologists like Prentice-Dunn have emphasised the importance of both private and public self-awareness in group situations. They argue that reduced attention to our private thoughts, feelings and attitudes is similar to being deindividuated. This state does not necessarily bring about anti-social behaviour though, unless certain expectations are in place, e.g. being part of a football crowd with a tradition of aggressive behaviour. Public self-awareness is how we wish to be seen by others and is reflected by, for example, our behaviour and dress-sense. Public self-awareness plays a big part in interpersonal behaviour such as attraction and affiliation, i.e. girl meets boy situations. In order to attract others we often change our public identity, by the use of clothes, cosmetics and other physical props such as the car we drive. Lack of public self-awareness can cause behaviour to be independent of **social norms** and therefore to translate into overtly aggressive behaviour. This might explain why some headlines are surprising, for example 'Yuppies in rioting crowd'. Why are we surprised? The projected image of a yuppie is that of a middle-class, clean-cut, successful individual, not someone who would be part of a mob. We commonly associate mobs with football fans or urban youths.

Answer the following either verbally or in written note form:

1 Define the difference between individuation and deindividua-tion.
2 Describe in detail one of the studies as evidence of the process of deindividuation.
3 Describe how role expectation might be an explanation for the results achieved by researchers such as Festinger and Zimbardo?

Progress exercise

Social identity theory (SIT)

Reicher and Potter (1985) proposed that one aspect of crowd behaviour, which had been ignored by many, was the fact that collective behaviour is also an inter-group phenomenon. As we saw above with Marsh's study of football fans, there is a clear-cut confrontational rivalry between two distinct groups: home team and away team supporters. Even if the rivalry does not result in aggressive behaviour it is often expressed in symbolic form such as ritualised aggression. Social identity theory can be of help in explaining this in so far as it draws a distinction between our **personal** and social **identity**. Our personal identity consists of those aspects of self which are idiosyncratic and peculiar to ourselves. They become replaced with the shared social identity of the crowd, e.g. United supporter (red scarves) as opposed to being a City supporter (blue scarves). Social identity theorists point to the evidence that many collectives are there for a very specific shared purpose, e.g. to support a team or to protest against blood sports. Within the groups there will be, therefore, a high degree of shared social identity. This in turn promotes **social categorisation** of self and others in terms of the nature and purpose of the group.

What is meant by this is that as a person I am male, a worker and a father (personal identity), but as a member of a football crowd I become a United supporter (my shared identity). This wider group identity will define and limit behaviour, i.e. promote conformity to shared ways of behaving. As we saw in chapter 2, many laboratory studies seem to show that conformity to small group norms can be obtained in about a third of participants. Research into group behaviour also points to the presence of the phenomenon known as **group mind**, i.e. the way people seem to adopt a qualitatively different mode of thinking when a member of a group than when not a member of a group. So, this will provide the group with general norms as to how to behave but will not necessarily help in a specific or unusual event, such as happened at Hillsborough.

Reicher and Potter (1985) maintain that this is what happened in the St Paul's district of Bristol in 1980. St Paul's is a community in a deprived area of Bristol with high unemployment and a high degree of social deprivation. The local police raided a café one morning on a tip-off that illegal drinking was taking place. As they tried to leave, bricks were thrown, and they called for back up. By the time it had arrived, a crowd, estimated to be about three thousand, had begun to riot. Reicher's analysis of events revealed that far from being a Le Bon 'mob', the crowd was very selective in their destructive endeavours. Vehicles were overturned and set alight and some property was damaged. But Reicher pointed to a number of important elements:

- Aggression seemed only to be against authority/establishment symbols, e.g. the police, banks.
- Rioters were not unrestrained in their behaviour but selective.
- The rioting remained within the confines of the district of St Paul's and did not spread to other parts of Bristol. (Similar events had been observed in the 1980s in other cities such as Manchester and Liverpool.)
- Damage to other property and cars seemed to be because the cars were thought to be unmarked police cars or property belonging to police sympathisers.

After the event, rioters and residents informed interviewers that they felt a strong sense of social identity with their community and its members.

Answer the following either verbally or in written note form:

1 Think of a recent example of a rioting crowd and using the information contained in the section on deindividuation try to explain it.
2 Using the same example as in 1 explain the riot using social identity theory.

Progress exercise

Methodological problems

The example above, the St Paul's riot, illustrates well the methodological problems researchers have in studying collective behaviour. As an observer on the sidelines, for example, how unbiased would a participant be? Suppose we interview rioters who took part, as opposed to those who watched, could we rely on their eyewitness evidence? Many would point to the studies in **confabulation**, which seem to show that we often adapt our memories to suit our existing expectations (Loftus and Loftus, 1975).

In addition, Kruglanski (1980) showed that confabulation has a further dimension, rigidity, in that despite incontrovertible evidence to the contrary some participants will 'freeze' on to an explanation of events which is untrue. What we think we saw in an emotional state may be very different to what we recall later. This could be a conscious act or it could be a defence mechanism to make the anxiety of the experience more bearable.

That leaves only one other alternative, to try and conduct a controlled experiment. Leaving the ethical considerations to one side for the moment, how feasible would it be to panic a group of unsuspecting participants while at the same time having a similar crowd in a similar situation who do not experience panic? The project has already been tried. French (1944) locked participants in a room and then tried to panic them by introducing smoke into the room and sounding the alarm. One group broke down the door and knocked over the smoke generator. Another group pondered whether their reactions were being observed. This clearly illustrates the problem in replicating real-life situations in a laboratory. At the same time there is the question of how ethical is it to deliberately panic or make angry a group of volunteer participants? To perform the experiment you would have to ignore a number of guidelines, e.g. obtaining full and informed consent, recommended by professional bodies such as the **BPS**.

An alternative to this would be to conduct interviews as did Benewick and Holton (1987). As we have already pointed out in other sections, there are methodological flaws in this in so far as the interviewer can influence eyewitness testimony and, in addition to that, there is the problem of interviewee bias.

Summary

This chapter has concerned itself with social interaction in crowds. Such behaviour is difficult to study since as a social scientist you may only have at your disposal biased media newsreel and some first-hand accounts from demonstrators, many, if not all, of whom will not be used to making scientific observations. Much of the information gathered will be qualitative and will not lend itself to thorough experimental investigation. But from this seemingly impossible situation some distinct explanations have emerged. As yet we are not in a position to decide whether one should take precedence over the others, but that in itself will, I hope, keep you as fascinated as I am by this phenomenon.

Social psychologists include fads, cults, demonstrations as well as rioting crowds within the area of collective behaviour. Le Bon and Durkheim saw crowd behaviour as sometimes leading to social unrest and sometimes, in the case of the peaceful crowd, contributing to social cohesion. Early theorists, such as Le Bon, have been criticised because they were unscientific. Later theorists, such as Marsh, point to the fact that some crowd behaviour is governed by rules. Waddington contends that demonstrations and riots are complex and require explanation on a number of levels. Deindividuation is a further contemporary explanation. Reicher and Potter proposed that one aspect of collective behaviour, which had not been examined closely, was inter-group behaviour. They proposed SIT as an explanation. There are a number of methodological problems in studying crowd behaviour.

Think about the following crowds:

- market day
- political demonstration
- a panicking crowd
- hysterical adoring fans

Choose an approach, such as Waddington's, and try to explain the collective behaviour.

Review exercise

Further reading

Hogg, M. A. and Vaughan, G. M. (1995) *Social Psychology: An Introduction*, Hemel Hempstead: Prentice Hall/Harvester Wheatsheaf. This is a very thorough text on social psychology with sections on collective behaviour and crowds. In addition, both authors are keen on diagrammatic models. So, if you prefer a picture to a verbal explanation, this is the book to do follow-up work from.

Manstead, A. and Hewstone, M. (eds) (1995) *The Blackwell Encyclopaedia of Social Psychology*, Oxford: Blackwell. This is a book worth buying only if you intend to study this aspect of psychology at university. It contains much information related to this topic and each theory is explained in detail.

5

Leadership and followers

Introduction

You can tell that an idea or concept has had an impact on a society by the way it has entered the language and communication we use. For example, the words 'leader' and 'follower' can be seen in sayings such as: 'lead article', 'leading from the front', 'follow like sheep', 'loss leader'. An examination of these sayings and epithets reveals an obvious attitudinal distinction. We tend to regard leading and leadership as positive and following or being organised by others as a lesser state; it is often used negatively to imply a lack of determination or independence.

Defining leadership is difficult but it is often easy to recognise. In terms of influence, we could look at leadership as the ultimate in minority influence.

In the words of Reber (1985) 'to function as a leader is to manifest leadership'. And a leader is: 'Anyone who holds a position of dominance, authority or influence in a group.'

Great person theory

The theory proposes that leaders possess key personality traits and other unique characteristics which predestine them to lead (Hook, 1955).

Early anthropological studies seemed to confirm this, i.e. those at the top, 'leaders of the pack', had greater skill at hunting, fighting or food gathering making them, therefore, 'natural leaders'.

It was argued that because these 'natural leaders' are so fundamentally different from followers and because followers do not in the main have their characteristics, leaders are therefore able to influence others. It was believed that these (traits) remain constant over a lifetime. It was further believed that all great leaders possess the same qualities irrespective of the historical period in which they lived or their culture. On the basis of this assumption, therefore, an examination of personalities as diverse as Hitler, Martin Luther King, Alexander the Great, Jesus and Hannibal would reveal them to have had more similarities than differences.

A typical study from this period was carried out by Randle (1956). Randle interviewed and gave psychological tests to 1,427 executives from 27 USA companies in order to identify personality traits and abilities which it was assumed would cluster in leaders but not followers. Thirty traits were identified, such as the need for achievement, motivation and intelligence, in order to differentiate good, poor and mediocre leaders. Basically, Randle found that good leaders were more intelligent and more motivated than poor leaders.

In general, the search for personality traits, which predispose individuals to leadership, has been unsuccessful. Correlations between individual traits such as extroversion and leadership and correlations among traits such as, say, motivation and intelligence and leadership have produced very low relationships (Yukl, 1981). An analysis of pooled results shows that traits that correlate weakly with leadership are in the main a tendency to be above average in intelligence, self-confidence, talkativeness and a need to be dominant. Leaders, according to this theory anyway, also tend to enjoy good health, and be attractive and tall.

In some reviews the opinion is that even with intelligence the correlations are so weak that this ability cannot be seen as an overwhelming qualification for leadership.

Evaluation and commentary

The problem with the great person perspective and its reliance on personality factors is threefold:

1   As the relationship is so low, it could be that the correlation is there only by chance. In any case, correlation studies can only claim to show a relationship, they are not a demonstration of cause and effect.
2   Having identified 'the leader', we often attribute personality traits to explain their success, i.e. we commit the **fundamental attribution error. Attribution theory** (Heider, 1958) states that when explaining our own and other people's actions, we often resort to dispositional (internal) or situational (external) explanations. If I see someone crying do I choose to say they are 'soft' and looking for attention (internal), or do I look for a cause in the immediate environment (situational). The error comes in tending to ignore situational causes of behaviour and relying on dispositional causes. In the case of leaders we often ignore situational factors, such as the events that led to their rise to power, and prefer to look to internal factors, describing them as 'brilliant' leaders pitted against an enemy.
3   Taking it that the relationship does exist, however weakly, then how are we to decide if the traits identified make good leaders or whether leaders adopt these traits once they have become leaders?

Taxonomies

In the past social scientists resorted to compiling lists or sets of attributes and principles, i.e. **taxonomies**, that they felt constituted leadership behaviour. Such attributes include things like power.

Progress exercise

Answer the following either verbally or in written note form:

1 Describe the trait ('great person') perspective.
2 What are the weaknesses in this approach?
3 What is the fundamental attribution error and how does it work in relation to how we view leaders?

The sociologist Weber (1921), one of the earliest observers of leadership behaviour, hypothesised that a leader's authority came from one or all of three sources:

- rational, resting on the assumption that leaders represent legitimate roles and norms;
- traditional, resting on the belief that leaders represent the continuity of accepted social order;
- charismatic, arising from the individual characteristics of the leader or what we might define today as the 'cult' of leadership.

The latter has often been associated with leaders who are perceived to have 'greatness' or 'presence' as described above in the great person perspective. Charismatic leaders, because of their determination, energy and abilities, are often associated with power. This is further reinforced in so far as they seem able to persuade large groups of individuals to follow them regardless, on some occasions, of their personal safety. In addition they often appear to change political, social or economic reality for their followers.

Others since have offered similar taxonomies, the most quoted being that of Collins and Raven (1969). They identified six forms of social power of which some are held by leaders or may be held by other members of a group:

- reward power – the power to bestow rewards;
- coercive power – the power to punish;
- referent power – achieved as a result of individuals wishing to identify with the individual seen as in the lead;

- expert power – this arises as a result of one member of the group having a greater knowledge than others;
- legitimate power – power as a result of social position;
- informational power – power as a result of holding on to or knowing particular valued information.

Let us examine more closely one of these: expert power. This is often seen in many everyday activities, with which the reader will be familiar, where leadership is an aspect. Student–teacher, supervisor–worker or tour guide–tourist are common examples. As a member of a touring group, the guide has the power of greater knowledge and experience and, as a consequence, few question their authority. So, when the guide issues a warning or instruction we invariably heed it.

Evaluation

The problem with taxonomies is that they are a list or summary and are often theoretical, i.e. based on a particular view as to how societies work. They are frequently based on personal experience (case studies) or anecdotal evidence (unregulated observations). Essentially, therefore, they are non-experimental and as evidence are considered useful, but of low quality, i.e. they are difficult to generalise from to other situations. Having said that they often provide psychologists with a starting point from which to examine other aspects of leadership behaviour, e.g. style of leadership.

Leadership behaviour

The Lewin, Lippitt and White study

Assuming then that personality traits and abilities such as high intelligence are not prerequisites for success as a leader, perhaps the way a leader behaves is important. One of the most famous studies which manipulated leadership behaviour while at the same time observing changes in the behaviour of the followers was a study carried out by Lewin, Lippitt and White (1939). (This study is detailed in article 5 of the key research summaries in chapter 6. Read this now.)

In addition they conducted an extension of the experiment in which each confederate (leader) swapped groups and adopted the leadership role for that group, in other words each group was exposed to only one leadership style but enacted by three separate individuals. This allowed the experimenters to make the important distinction between leadership behaviour and personality. Each leader, irrespective of his personality, could, with apparent ease, adopt the three differing types of leadership. As a result of this, they were able to promote the idea that democratic styles of leadership were more beneficial.

Evaluation

Although this was a very structured study, carried out in a real as opposed to a laboratory environment, the study had no control, i.e. a group or groups taught by a leader adopting no particular leadership behaviour because they are not aware of the purpose of the study. The research did not take into consideration situational factors, e.g. communication between members of each group or the way the rooms were organised. As we will see in the next section the latter may have influenced the behaviour of both leader and follower alike. Similarly, we cannot assume that democratic styles are more beneficial since the criterion being used to assess leadership needs to be defined in the light of the task in hand. If group harmony were the goal of a leader then democratic leadership appears to be effective. If the goal of the group is productivity, then the autocratic leader's style is more effective (Smith and Peterson, 1988).

Progress exercise

Answer the following either verbally or in written note form:

1 How did Lewin *et al.* control for the influence each leader's personality might have on the group?
2 What does the research of Lewin *et al.* enable us to say about the role of personality factors and leadership?

Situational perspective

Do leaders just happen as a result of opportunity, i.e. right person, right qualities and right time? In contrast to the 'great person' perspective, psychologists have examined functional aspects of inter-action in groups to see if it has an influence on who emerges as a leader in a group.

Position in the group

Howells and Beker (1962), for example, showed that in experimental groups, situational aspects of the group as trivial as who sits at the head of a table can have an effect in determining who leads. The structure of a group, i.e. whether sat in a circle or in rows, may well influence who we choose as a leader, and as a consequence who will be a follower. Altemeyer and Jones (1974) demonstrated that the occupants of end seats at a rectangular table received most nominations as leaders. However, when participants are seated at a circular table, these differences decrease (Lécuyer, 1976). This would seem to show that positional aspects of how members of a group are physically organised in relation to each other could affect the emergence of a leader.

Changing situation

In a classic study often referred to as the Robber's Cave Experiment, Sherif *et al.* (Sherif, 1962) studied inter-group relationships between groups of boys at a summer camp. Initially the boys were separated into groups and kept apart in order to establish ingroup identity. Next they were brought together in order to play competitive games. This was done to reinforce ingroup identity and at the same time establish **outgroup** rejection. Finally, the boys were presented with a problem that only the whole group could solve. Sherif and his associates found that in a changed situation, the leadership choice changed. This seems to show that leadership may have more to do with the parameters of the situation, i.e. the task in hand, than the personality of the leader.

Communication within groups

Another study, which took the view that the situation may play a large part in creating a leader, carried out by Bavelas *et al.* (1965), investigated the relationship between talkativeness and leadership. Participants were sat in such a way that they could be involved in a discussion yet at the same time observe a red or green light. To facilitate discussion the experimenter explained that a flashing red light meant that their contribution was hampering the discussion. A green flashing light was to indicate that their contribution was considered to be very useful. He explained further that he might flash either light at a participant who was silent. Participants could not see each other's lights. After the discussion was under way the experimenters, by manipulating the red and green lights, targeted one of the quieter participants and were able to stimulate the quiet participant into talking more and eventually taking the lead in the discussion. After the experiment was over the participants were asked to rate each other in terms of traits such as leadership. It was discovered that the more the targeted participant spoke the higher s/he was rated on leadership qualities afterwards. This would seem to show that a situational factor, such as the amount a person says as a member of a group, might cast that person in a leadership role, irrespective of their personality.

Evaluation of situational explanations

These studies appear to have 'scientific' credibility because some are controlled studies. Many would criticise them, however, because they do not have ecological validity, i.e. they are not true to life. In real-world situations, many factors may influence why we follow one person rather than another, i.e. we are affected by both situational and dispositional influences. (As we saw in the Lewin *et al.* study, the behaviour of a leader can be influential in determining how followers behave.) It would be difficult to emulate this in a laboratory and at the same time remain true to life. Others criticise the studies on the grounds that they do not take into account other social influences, e.g. conformity, that may be responsible for one person becoming a leader whilst others in the same group do not.

Answer the following either verbally or in written note form.

1   List three situational factors that influence leadership choice.
2   Outline an experiment that tries to establish that situational factors are important in the emergence of a leader.
3   Explain why situational influences such as those described above may not be an adequate explanation as to why someone becomes a leader.

Leadership style

Leadership style is another avenue along which researchers have gone in order to explain what is complex interactive behaviour, involving leaders and followers. By examining styles of leadership behaviour, psychologists have been able to study the behaviour of followers and leaders. This is important since in relationships there is an interactive process; i.e. the behaviour of the leader will act as a stimulus for the behaviour of the follower(s), and vice versa: as we saw in the Lewin *et al.* study above. This is in contrast to constitutional, i.e. type and trait theories, which tend to examine personality and case history aspects of individuals considered to be leaders.

Task v. social-emotional specialists

A classic study by Bales and Slater (1955) in which they observed small discussion groups found that those who emerged as leaders fell into two basic categories:

*   task specialists, i.e. those who were predominantly concerned with the group achieving its goal;
*   social-emotional specialists, i.e. those who were predominantly concerned with relationships between group members.

Although Bales found that some could take on both roles, in the main two separate participants would take on each role within the group. This seems to show that specific leadership roles may emerge within a group, which might be part of the group dynamic.

79

A large leadership study conducted in Ohio (Fleishman, 1973) seems to confirm Bales' results. Questionnaires concerning the behaviour of leaders in mainly military and industrial establishments were given to participants to complete. The researchers identified two categories of leadership behaviour:

- initiating, i.e. managers or officers who were essentially goal- and **task-orientated**;
- consideration, i.e. managers or officers who were essentially relationship-orientated in so far as they were more concerned with promoting group harmony.

Whereas Bales felt that the distinction was an either/or situation, i.e. high scorers on task-orientated leadership roles were low scorers on socio-emotional specialism, the Ohio study seemed to show that leaders could score high or low on either aspect or in the case of some they scored high on both. Leadership style, therefore, may be dependent on far more complex social influences than whether a leader adopts one style of behaviour in preference to another.

Bass (1990) reviewed a wealth of literature on leadership and as well as noting the above listed the following as other conclusions:

- autocratic leadership styles are more effective in authoritarian environments;
- task-orientated leaders are more effective if circumstances are favourable or unfavourable rather than on an even level.

Evaluation

There have been many studies since which have tended to support the dual-leadership idea. In real life we often hear this idea expressed about various leaders: opinion may focus on whether the person is friendly and receptive to ideas (democratic) or whether they 'lead from the front' because of their firm conviction and inner strength (autocratic). But we must be cautious in accepting this interpretation above all others, e.g. trait theories. It could be that the reason task-orientated and socio-emotional specialists emerge in groups is because they have different personality characteristics. Similarly, situational aspects, such as the task the group was involved in, could also have a bearing on why one or the other emerges as the group leader. Studies, such as Bales', did not always take into consideration situational factors and therefore we have no way of knowing whether they were controlled for.

Finally we must not forget that much of the data collected comes from small group, laboratory-based research and as such they can be criticised for not having ecological validity.

Answer the following either verbally or in written note form:

1 What do psychologists mean by leadership style?
2 What is the difference between a task-specialist and socio-emotional specialist?
3 What criticism can be made in relation to this approach to the study of leadership?

Progress exercise

The contingency perspective

Many contemporary social psychologists feel an approach, which emphasises the interactive nature of group and leader behaviour is a better explanation. Contingency theories emerged from observations that effective leadership was not simply whether an individual leader 'had what it takes' (traits) or was in the 'right place at the right time' (situational) or was task-orientated (style). It was more to do with a mixture of parameters such as the nature of the group, e.g. engineers or artists, and what they were engaged in, e.g. crisis or planning meeting. A number of psychologists have offered contingency or transactional theories to try and explain the complexity of leader–subordinate interaction. The best known and researched is Fielder's theory.

Fielder's contingency theory

Fielder (1971, 1981) proposed that effective leadership was contingent (dependent) on three factors: the leader's relationship with his followers, the task and the leader's power. He accepted Bales' separation of styles into task- or socio-emotional (relationship) orientated leaders. He hypothesised further that leaders who are task-orientated, therefore, are authoritarian, directive and at times intolerant of group members who do not contribute. In contrast relationship-orientated leaders are relaxed and friendly and try to be on good terms with all group members irrespective of their effort, or lack of it.

Fielder was concerned also with the personality of the leader as measured by an instrument called the LPC Scale (least preferred co-worker). Testees were asked to think of all the co-workers they had been associated with that they liked the least. They were then asked to rate them for qualities such as friendliness. The rating scale consisted of eighteen bipolar sets of qualities, e.g. warm/cold, nice/nasty, friendly/unfriendly:

Nice ☐ ☐ ☐ ☐ ☐ ☐ ☐ ☐ Nasty

The scale is based on the assumption that participants who give negative ratings to their least preferred co-worker (low scorers) are essentially task-orientated, in that they are more concerned with getting the job done. Individuals who give ratings nearer to zero or even positive ratings to their least preferred co-worker (high scorers) are relatively relationship-orientated.

As to which one makes the best leader, contingency theorists would say that it depends (is contingent) on the leadership situation. In some situations, task-orientated leaders will be effective and in other situations they will be detrimental to group harmony and therefore the effectiveness of the group. In this situation, therefore, a relationship-orientated leader will be more useful. Above all, they contend, it will be contingent on the control the leader has.

As mentioned earlier situational control is dependent on three factors (in order of priority):

1   What the group has to accomplish, e.g. resolving a crisis, increasing productivity, etc. Tasks vary widely in so far as some are clearly defined, e.g. assemble an engine, whilst others are unclear, e.g. bring together culturally divergent protagonists (*task*).

2   Leader–group member relationships, e.g. whether the leader is liked/disliked or merely tolerated by the group (*socio-emotional relationship*).

3   The power and authority possessed by a leader, e.g. does s/he have the power to hire or fire or reward through remuneration. In the case of military leaders, their power is considerable in comparison to say an assistant floor manager of a supermarket (*power*).

On the basis of the above a leader could be assessed as either high or low on the three dimensions: relationships with followers, task and power. Fielder's model predicts that an individual who has good relations with subordinates, in a situation with a well-defined problem to solve and whose power and authority is legitimate will make a very effective leader. They would score high/high/high on the above dimensions. The reverse assessment, low/low/low, therefore, would be the least favourable situation to try to control. In the case of the latter the task would be poorly defined, the leader–group relations would be poor and the power and authority invested in the leader would be questionable.

These are ideal situations, of course. A more likely combination would be low/high/high, high/low/high, or other combinations which are intermediate ratings. Having pointed this out we are still left with the problem of who would make the best leader in an intermediate situation? In a poorly defined situation, for example, would a task-orientated leader with little 'real' power be better than a powerless relationship-orientated leader? Fielder believed that low LPC scorers, i.e. task-orientated leaders, would do well under low or high situational control. An autocratic style of leadership would bring structure to an ill-defined problem. Similarly, in a well-defined situation strong leadership, leading from the front, sets an example to subordinates and therefore helps establish the leader's power. High LPC scorers, i.e. relationship-orientated leaders, would do well in middle-range situations where relationships are moderately good, the problem is reasonably well defined and the power of the leadership is moderately legitimate.

Generally, the contingency theory of leadership has attracted a lot of research and is considered a worthwhile model in the analysis of leadership.

Empirical research

Chemers *et al.* (1985), for example, examined university administrators and divided them into task-orientated or relationship-orientated leaders. Their jobs were examined and sorted into those that were low, moderate or high in situational control. Low in situational control were jobs where: procedures were unclear, task demands were unpredictable and the administrator had little 'real' power. Similarly administrators with high situational control were those who had clear-cut procedures, well-defined tasks to complete and had power over the work of subordinates.

As a test of their effectiveness they were asked how much stress they experienced in carrying out their duties. The results are shown in Figure 1.

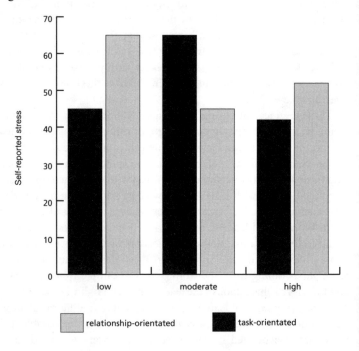

Figure 1 **Graph to show how stressful two types of leaders said they found situations which varied in the amount of control they had**

Source: After Chemers (1985)

As predicted by contingency theory, task-orientated leaders felt under most stress in situations where they had moderate control, i.e. neither overall nor little control. In contrast, relationship-orientated leaders felt the greatest stress when they had low control. Chemers collected other data from his administrators including details of stress-related health problems (e.g. angina, eczema). A difference emerged in that task-orientated leaders reported more illness than did relationship-orientated leaders in situations of moderate control. Relationship-orientated leaders reported more stress-related health problems in positions of low control.

Conclusion

We can conclude from these results that a leader's orientation is significant in relation to the control s/he has over a situation. This is important in the selection and training of officers and managers, in so far as task-orientated managers define tasks and tell people what to do. Some situations, such as trouble-shooting in times of a crisis, require this. The task-orientated leader/manager, if s/he is effective, will quickly define what has to be done, divide it into sub-tasks and tell subordinates how and what to do. As a result of this they gain the respect of their followers and a boost to their power. Where a workforce or group has a history of discord and low morale a relationship-orientated leader would be better in so far as they will try to harmonise the group by, for example, allowing them to air grievances. This in turn leads to an increase in how subordinates perceive the power of this type of leader.

Current trends in business seem to be taking this on board. Managers and executives with specific skills are increasingly being hired on short-term contracts. Some will be task-orientated and will be hired to get a job done against a tight deadline, such as the installing of a new computerised system to deal with a customer and product database. Others will be relationship-orientated and will be employed to say set up a team in a department of the civil service to introduce, pilot and implement new legislation.

Criticism

Fielder based his theory on the controversial evidence of Bales. Many would say that Bales' original experiment lacked **validity** since it was a laboratory-based research into group behaviour.

Fielder's measuring instrument itself has its critics, too. As emphasised in other chapters, data obtained from questionnaires, rating scales and surveys are considered to be low in terms of validity, in comparison say to measurement of temperature. This can be measured more precisely because it is interval data, i.e. measured on a scale of fixed units. I know that 4° C is twice as much as 2° C. In using a rating scale we are attempting to measure subjective variables objectively. Unfortunately if I rate a person as friendly at point 2 on the above scale I cannot be certain that a person who has been rated at 4 on the same scale is twice as friendly. In this respect, a rating scale is low in reliability. Rice (1978) tested the LPC and found low test–retest reliability. This means that as a measuring instrument it cannot be relied upon to be consistent.

Fielder assumed also that the leader's style would be consistent across both time and situation and this may not be true. Argyle's work (Argyle, 1971) on non-verbal communication and social interaction seems to show that our behaviour in groups is much more changeable than was thought by earlier theorists such as Freud and Jung. Argyle seems to be saying that we may well have a basic personality which can be labelled as extrovert but that in groups our behaviour will be as influenced by the people we are with as by our personality. Lewin *et al.*, mentioned earlier, were able to show that it was quite easy for leaders to adopt any of the three styles of leadership: democratic, autocratic or laissez-faire. It could be that both situational and leader–group behaviour vary and require not a single style but a variety of styles, i.e. the best leaders might be those who can constantly adapt to a changing situation.

Finally, although Fielder's contingency theory does examine the interaction between the leader as a person and situational factors such as the task to be achieved it does not address other social influences that affect interaction in groups such as leader–follower expectation or obedience. In other words, there is a dynamic relationship between followers and leaders, i.e. without a relationship with subordinates or followers there cannot be a leader.

Answer the following either verbally or in written note form:

1   What do you understand by the term contingency theories?
2   List and describe situational factors noted by Fielder which he considered were important in leader–follower relationships.
3   Compare and contrast the leadership styles of task-orientated and relationship-orientated leaders.
4   Describe two criticisms you can make of Fielder's theory.

Followers

Leaders have been brought down by their followers on many occasions. Being a follower, therefore, is by no means a position of powerlessness. What interests social psychologists is the form this mutual influence takes. As mentioned already, Fielder, Lewin and Bales have all noted that different styles of leadership can affect followers.

Expectancy effects

An **expectancy effect** is the idea that we come to many situations with a mental set, i.e. a framework of ideas about that situation, so that we anticipate or 'expect' a certain type of behaviour. Our mental set will be based on many aspects of ourselves including our personality and past experiences. In relation to follower–leader interaction our expectations of each differs. If you examine your stereotypes for different groups in society your stereotype for 'worker' will probably be very different to your stereotype for 'executive'.

Leader–follower interaction may be influenced by the **self-fulfilling prophecy**, i.e. an individual's beliefs about another person, or group, might elicit from them behaviour that confirms the initial expectation. If I believe my workers are lazy they may in turn behave in ways which confirm my view of them. In contrast if I expect 100% from my followers they may exhibit behaviour which confirms that perception of them.

Many researchers have investigated the process whereby individuals or groups seem able to elicit behaviour from others which seems to confirm the expectation we have of them, e.g. low-ability students, hostile partners, extroverts, etc.

Rosenthal and Jacobson (1968) conducted a classic study in this by administering an IQ test to a group of primary school children. Their teachers were told that the test results were a reliable indicator of future excellence. In fact, the test was a standardised test of general intelligence. The teachers were given the names of the children who were identified as having potential for 'an unusual forward spurt of academic progress'. In fact, the children were selected at random. Having given the teachers 'expectations', the researchers predicted that these would be fulfilled, despite being based on false information. When the children were re-tested a year later the prediction had largely come true, i.e. those children identified to the teachers as about to make significant progress had scored higher on the test than their classmates.

Applied to leader–follower relations it could be that workers and subordinates play out the expectations of their managers. McGregor (1960) proposed something very similar with reference to manager–subordinate relationships. Taken together with the idea of social expectation, the manager's view of his workforce may be as important in determining how subordinates behave as other factors, such as personality and leadership style. He contended that managers held two views of their workers:

- Theory X. Workers were lazy and worked only if they had to and therefore needed to be coerced into working harder.
- Theory Y. Workers could enjoy their work and would work hard if shown appreciation. The leader's role therefore was one of guidance and encouragement.

Expectancy confirmation sequence

Darley and Fazio (1980) have termed the process whereby we come to exhibit the behaviour expected of us as the expectancy confirmation sequence. If we examine this in terms of manager–worker relations the sequence can be represented as:

1   Manager believes that workers are lazy.
2   Manager behaves towards workers as if they are lazy.

3 Workers interpret manager's behaviour as one of mistrust/disrespect.
4 Workers' behaviour is constrained by the manager such that they find it difficult to behave in a manner other than to be indolent.
5 Workers seem to be behaving to expectation.

Empirical support

This sequence has been confirmed by many studies, such as Snyder and Swann (1978). They informed their participants that their partner in a competitive game was either hostile or non-hostile. Those who were in the hostile partnership behaved in a much more competitive way that those in the non-hostile partnership.

Hollander and Julian (1969) reviewed research on leadership and found that one of the recurrent themes in the literature was concerned with the importance of the leader's expectations of his/her followers. According to Hollander good leaders are those who have high expectations of their teams and who provide realistic goals. In contrast, low-performing and low-achieving teams of subordinates are often led by ineffectual leaders who do not have high expectations. This is confirmed by Bass (1990). He reviewed literature on leadership and concluded that productivity and follower satisfaction was in part dependent upon the expectations about leader behaviour.

There are limits to the self-fulfilling prophecy. Holtgraves *et al.* (1989) asked participants to observe a conversation between two males:

- half the participants believed that the two men were co-workers (expectation)
- the other half of the participants were led to believe they were worker and 'boss' (expectation).

In a clever twist to the study, both males were instructed by the researcher to behave as if they were co-workers; or one of them was told to behave like the boss of the other one.

The results of the study seem to show that non-verbal and verbal behaviour was as important as the expectation. In other words if the participants believed one of the men was a boss (expectation) and he acted like one (verbal and non-verbal cues) then they perceived him as

89

the 'boss' and by implication believed the other to be a subordinate. If on the other hand the person they expected to behave like a boss had verbal and non-verbal behaviour of a subordinate they were less sure of the relationship between the two.

Evaluation

There has been criticism of this research. Many point to the dubious ethics of the studies, i.e. not informing the participants fully of the aims of the studies. Many of the studies are not controlled and therefore cannot claim to show cause and effect. In addition, some of the studies are laboratory studies although the Rosenthal study can claim ecological validity as it was conducted in a naturalistic setting. There is also the **enlightenment effect**, i.e. as the theory of the expectancy effects has become popular, in turn it has come to influence the behaviour of both participants and researchers. Some would argue that the only effective research which can be done now or in the future would have to involve a double blind condition since the concept of self-fulfilling prophecy has to an extent largely entered the daily life of Western cultures.

Hollander (1985) points also to the fact that expectations are not consistent either on the part of leaders or followers. Where workers or subordinates have performed well in the past they may be expected to again, despite changes which may have occurred, e.g. changes in the composition of the group. Sorrentino and Field (1986) showed that in laboratory groups, group members who scored high on both task and socio-emotional dimensions of Bales' system were elected as leaders. This seems to indicate, in laboratory groups anyway, that followers prefer a more participatory style of management. Some leaders may not have the skills for this and therefore, through their behaviour, may exhibit the wrong expectations. This in turn may contribute to leader–follower dissonance resulting in poor relations between managers and workers. At the same time it may put follower against follower with one group feeling as if they are an outgroup while another group may feel as if they are an ingroup. As we have pointed out elsewhere (see p. 77) in/outgroup attitudes tend to distance groups from each other by creating ingroup cohesion and outgroup rejection, i.e. an 'us and them' mentality.

It would appear then that leader–follower behaviour is not a one-way process and neither is it fixed. On the evidence it would appear that it is at least a two-way process of mutual influence. To understand one or the other or both, therefore, the dual relationship between leader and follower must be understood in terms of group behaviour.

Answer the following either verbally or in written note form:

1 With reference to leader–follower behaviour, outline the expectancy confirmation sequence.
2 Define the self-fulfilling prophecy and describe a study that seems to show this.
3 Why might the expectancy effect not be consistent in leader–follower relations?

Progress exercise

Summary

Early researchers looked for a correlation between personality traits and leadership. Other researchers looked to situational factors as a means to explain leadership, e.g. seating position. Others examined leadership behaviour, e.g. Lewin *et al.*, and yet others produced taxonomies of power and leadership. Bales and Slater found that in laboratory groups distinct leaders emerge: task specialists or socio-emotional specialists. Others point to the fact that leader–follower relationships are complex. Contingency theories try to address this, e.g. Fielder's. Expectancy effects, such as the self-fulfilling prophecy, may influence leader–follower relations. Many believe that leader–follower relationships are dynamic, two-way processes.

Review exercise

Look at the research/concept on the left and with the aid of the glossary and the chapter try and produce a few key words to summarise it. The first one has been completed for you.

Research/Concept	Key word
Expectation	Mental set – anticipate behaviour
Situational factors	
Lewin *et al.* (1939)	
Expectancy confirmation sequence	
Bales and Slater (1955)	
Fundamental attribution error	
Theory X	
LPC Scale	
Type and trait theories	
Socio-emotional specialists	
Contingency theory	

Further reading

Bass, B. M. (1990) *Bass and Stogdill's Handbook of Leadership: Theory, Research and Managerial Applications*, 3rd edition, New York: Free Press. As the title implies this is a specialist book and is full of examples and studies concerned with leaders and their relationship with followers and subordinates.

Deaux, K. and Wrightsman, L. S. (1988) *Social Psychology*, 5th edition, Brooks/Cole Publishing. This book has a good chapter on leadership which also contains sub-sections on leadership and gender and leadership and followers.

Study aids

IMPROVING YOUR ESSAY WRITING SKILLS

At this point in the book, you have acquired the knowledge necessary to tackle the exam itself. Answering examination questions is a skill and in this chapter I hope to help you improve this skill. As examiners, we have some ideas about what goes wrong in exams. Most importantly students do not provide the kind of evidence the examiner is looking for. A grade C answer is typically accurate and is reasonably constructed but has limited detail and commentary. To lift such an answer to grade A or B may require no more than fuller detail, better use of material and a coherent organisation. By studying the essays presented in this chapter, and the examiner's comments, you can learn how to turn your grade C answer into grade A. Please note that marks given by the examiners in the practice essays should be used as a guide only and are not definitive. They represent the 'raw marks' given by an AEB examiner. That is, the marks the examiner would give to the examining board based on a total of 24 marks per question broken down into Skill A (description) and Skill B (evaluation). Tables showing the scheme are in Appendix C of Paul Humphreys' title in this series, *Exam Success in AEB Psychology*. They may not be the marks given on the examination certificate received ultimately by the student because all examining boards are required to use a common standardised system called the Uniform Mark Scheme (UMS) which adjusts all raw scores to a single standard acceptable to all examining boards.

The essays are about the length a student would be able to write in 35–40 minutes (leaving you extra time for planning and checking). Each essay is followed by detailed comments about the strengths and weaknesses of the essay. The most common problems to look out for are:

- Failure to answer the actual question set and presenting 'one written during your course'.
- A lack of evaluation, or commentary – many weak essays suffer from this.
- Too much evaluation and not enough description. Description is vital in demonstrating your knowledge and understanding of the selected topic.
- Writing 'everything you know' in the hope that something will get credit. Excellence is displayed through selectivity, and therefore improvements can often be made by *removing* material which is irrelevant to the question set.

For more ideas on how to write good essays you should consult *Exam Success in AEB Psychology* (Paul Humphreys) in this series.

Practice essay 1

Describe and evaluate research findings relating to conformity. (24 marks) [AEB 1998]

Candidate's answer

Crutchfield described conformity as yielding to group pressure. It's like doing what others want when really you wanted to do something different. Investigations into conformity have mainly centred on lab experiments.

Sherif investigated conformity. He placed participants in a darkened room with a spot of light at the end. If you look at the light for a while, it begins to move. This is known as the autokinetic effect. It happens naturally because the eye is moving the entire time even when you are staring. Sherif found that when the participants were in pairs their estimates as to how far the light had moved were much closer than when they were estimating on their own. In other words, they seem to have based their estimates on what others in the group thought.

Asch criticised this experiment because there was no absolute measure of the autokinetic effect. It's different for different people. He carried out a series of experiments using apparatus such as:

Stimulus card   test lines

Participants had to say which of the lines a, b, c, were like the test line. He placed his participants in groups. What the participant did not know was that the others in the group were in league with the experimenter Asch. He had primed them to agree that line (a) was like the test line rather than line (b). In this way Asch was able to measure conformity more precisely than Sherif. On some occasions, the participants agreed with the confederates. They contradicted the evidence from their own eyes. Asch experimented further with other variations and found that the size and composition of the groups could affect the amount of conformity. So, if the group had a lot of confederates in it and they were say college teachers or vicars then there was more accuracy. If there was a small number of confederates or if the participant had a partner, then there was less conformity. He and others also found that to bring about the maximum group pressure a group of between 3 to 5 was needed. Larger than 7 did not seem to make much difference.

Crutchfield criticised Asch's experiments and designed his own. He put his participants in booths with coloured lights that signalled right or wrong answers to questions such as:

Which has the greater area?

A star   or a circle?

What his participants did not know was that the choices of other participants in the other booths had been rigged to look as if they had made the wrong choice. Like Asch he was able to bring about group pressure and like Asch he found conformity.

One of the criticisms you can make of all of these experiments is that they were done in the fifties. It could be that people in the fifties were more conformist than nowadays. Today we have more freedom and the role of women in society has changed. Another criticism you can make is that most of these experiments were done with male participants. It could be that if women students or mixed groups were used different results would have been achieved. Also there is the question of ecological validity. All of these experiments were conducted in a laboratory, which is not like real life.

Other experimenters have conducted similar experiments in the eighties and have not achieved the same degree of conformity. One experiment used engineering participants and did not achieve the same level of conformity as Asch. It was criticised however for the fact that engineering students were not a good choice of participant because of their training in measurement and mathematics.

Milgram did a series of experiments in which he compared the degree of conformity in different cultures. He found that cultures differ in the degree to which they will conform. But like Asch he found a similar degree of conformity.

Kelman and others feel that what Asch observed as conformity can be explained in other ways. Kelman distinguished between conformity, compliance and internalisation. He pointed to the fact that on being debriefed Asch's participants talked of conforming but wanting to disagree. In other words they were outwardly conforming but inwardly in disagreement. Kelman says this is qualitatively different to conformity.

It would appear then that there is a lot of experimental evidence to say that as humans we have a tendency to conform. Unfortunately this evidence is laboratory evidence and therefore does not have ecological validity.

Examiner's comment

This essay is likely to score around 15 out of 24 (9 for skill A + 6 for skill B); i.e. it is probably just about a B essay. The essay is reasonable but limited in terms of description and evaluation. This is because in some parts it is not descriptive enough, more detail is needed, and overall a slightly limited range of findings are described. In addition the evaluation although quite good could do with more elaboration.

It could have been improved in so far as the work of Milgram could have been described in greater detail, e.g. the fact that the two cultures were French and Norwegian and that the task was the judgement of tones. The criticisms at the end need developing. It is not sufficient to just say that an experiment or study lacks ecological validity. You need to say why and then for a very good mark suggest an alternative solution or way(s) of achieving a better result. In the case of this essay you need to say that the problem with conducting social psychology experiments is that they do not fully represent what may be happening in society. You could also point out that a psychological experiment in itself is a social situation and therefore subject to all the social and group pressures which affect us when in society.

Another aspect that would have taken this essay out of the B band would have been evaluation through inclusion of an alternative explanation such as a Freudian explanation. You could explain conforming behaviour as a defence mechanism; in order to cope with the anxiety of being non-conformist we identify with our fellows.

Similarly at the outset of the essay the definition could have been improved by the inclusion of the words: 'as perceived by us'. The terms, compliance and internalisation need defining too. Kelman's ideas could have been developed further to show that what has been called conformity by Asch and Crutchfield may have different aspects.

97

Practice essay 2

    (a) **Outline two theories of leadership. (12 marks)**

    (b) **Assess the extent to which these theories are supported by research evidence. (12 marks)**   **[AEB 1998]**

Candidate's answer

(a) In the past psychologists tended to believe that leaders had characteristics that were different to those of followers or subordinates (Great Person Approach). These personality characteristics were thought to be common to all leaders and that their development could be seen in childhood. In other words if you were to look at the personality traits of historic leaders as different as Hitler and Churchill you would find more similarities than differences.

More contemporary social scientists have tended to concentrate on situational factors; e.g. that leaders may be opportunists or a combination of environmental factors conspire to enable some to take up leadership roles while others get ignored. An examination of the situation surrounding a person's rise to power often reveals a degree of luck and opportunity. Hitler for example, it is acknowledged by historians, was in the right place at the right time in that he was a politician at the time of great turmoil in Germany.

Much research has been done on small groups and the ways in which leaders of these groups emerge. Group research seems to show that group members often fall into three categories:

- Task-orientated, i.e. people who want to get the task done
- Relation-orientated, i.e. group members who are more interested in group harmony
- Self-orientated, i.e. members who seem indifferent to the goals of the group and may even pervert group goals if they feel threatened by them.

(b) A lot of research was done to try and find correlations between personality traits such as extroversion and determination and leadership. These studies seemed to have proved little, except that generally leaders are often intelligent, tall, in good health and attractive. Yukl reviewed literature and found that the correlations are weak. This means that they are probably there by chance. Typical research in this area would be to give managers a personality test and in addition have their subordinates rate them for their leadership qualities. The psychologist would then look for traits that correlate with whether they were rated as good managers, bad managers or were mediocre. Such correlations are often weak, e.g. as low as 0.4, indicating that the relationship is only found in about 16% of cases. Many would consider this as too low to be sure that individuals in leadership positions have personality traits which are different from their subordinates.

In relation to situational factors, Bavelas conducted a typical experiment. Participants were sat in such a way that they could see lights. One light meant they were contributing to the group discussion. Another light meant they were not contributing well and a flashing light meant that they were too quiet. By manipulating the lights Bavelas was able to target a quiet participant and get him or her to lead the discussion. This showed that talkativeness could be a factor in who we choose to be our leader. Other researchers have conducted similar experiments of laboratory groups, and have found that emergent leaders can result from many aspects of group behaviour. Bass reviewed a mountain of literature in this area and noted that situational factors as different as: where you were sitting, the shape of the table participants sit at, how much you said, and the size of the group all contributed to whether you were chosen as a leader.

The problem with situational factors is that they are so diverse it is difficult to know which factors are the main aspects involved in the choice of a leader. Similarly, it is hard to control for personality and gender aspects that may be contributing to the emergence of a leader. Many of the studies were conducted in a laboratory and therefore lack ecological validity. This means that they are not representative of real life.

Another researcher found for example that personality traits were as important as the situation the leader found him/herself in. This researcher studied generals, and the outcome of the battles they participated in. Fielder (contingency theory) also said that good leadership was contingent upon personality factors and in addition other important things such as the power of the leader and the type of problem to be solved or the nature of the task. Researchers who have based their investigations on Fielder's theory have found, for example, that good leadership is often based on more than the situation the manager finds him/herself in or the type of person they are. The relationship between say, a manager and his workforce will depend on a two-way relationship, the type of problem to be addressed and the expectations leaders and followers have of each other. Clearly, this shows that the Great Person approach or group studies of situational factors, on their own, are inadequate as an explanation.

Examiner's comment

Part (a) is quite weak and would only score about 6 marks out of 12. This is because the question asks the candidate to outline two theories whereas the candidate has described aspects of both the 'great person' theory and research into situational factors affecting the emergence of a leader in laboratory research. The last part of the answer actually introduces three theories of leadership. The examiner will mark all three and the best two will be credited.

An 'outline' requires breadth rather than descriptive detail; although some description may be necessary to complete an adequate outline of a theory. It appears that the candidate may well be writing an answer they have prepared in advance in the hope that they may get some marks.

Part (b) is fair in attempting to assess the evidence but it is also vital to address the evidence you have quoted and explain how it supports, or does not support, the theory outline in part (a). This second part therefore could have been improved by clarifying points made more thoroughly, e.g. that correlation studies and personality questionnaires have weaknesses. The point made at the end, about expectation, could have been developed much more to include an assessment of the self-fulfilling prophecy. Similarly, evidence for situational factors could have been developed further, e.g. the point made about ecological validity. In addition, the whole essay could have been further improved by structuring it so that studies described in section (b) were shown to support/not support the theories of leadership described in section (a).

This section would probably have scored around 8 marks out of 12, giving a total of 14 marks out of 24, which is likely to be equivalent to a grade C.

KEY RESEARCH SUMMARIES

Article 1

'Behavioural study of obedience', S. Milgram in *Journal of Abnormal and Social Psychology* (1963) 67, 371–8

AIM   Milgram was interested in the nature of obedience to authority. He conducted a number of experiments in which he attempted to get people to punish other participants by the use of a graduating electrical shock, e.g. starting at 15 volts and ending in 450 volts (an electric shock which would be fatal for many people). The conduct of the experiment was intriguing although now it would be considered unethical.

METHOD   The 40 participants in his original study were recruited through a newspaper advertisement, which asked for volunteers to be involved in a 'study of memory'. Potential recruits were offered $4.50 per hour and the advertisement went on to say that no special training was needed. The advert then proceeded to list employement categories from which Milgram would like his volunteers to come. 'Factory workers, Businessmen, Construction workers, Clerks' and so on. He further specified that college students need not apply and that participants must be between 20 and 50 years of age. He was trying to recruit naïve participants.

The experiments were carried out, at first, at Yale University, a highly prestigious establishment and equivalent to Oxford or Cambridge in England.

To the naïve participants the procedure was fairly straightforward. They were introduced to another participant, referred to as the 'learner'. The participants were referred to as the 'teacher'. They were both told that the purpose of the experiment was to study the effects of punishment on learning. The teacher's task was to test the memory of his (they were all male) learner. If the learner got the answer wrong, the teacher was to administer an electric shock via a piece of apparatus in front of him with switches indicating the dosage. Beneath each switch was an indication of the strength of each dose, e.g. mild, severe. The final one had simply 'XXX' below it.

In the initial trial, Milgram placed the learner in an adjoining room, so that the teacher could not see him. The experiment proceeded and after a while the learner began to get some of the exercises wrong. The teacher was instructed to administer a shock. In the early stages of each trial there was no response from the learner but as the shocks got higher the learner began to moan and at more than 200 volts protested, at one point demanding to be released from the experiment. At 300 volts the learner banged on the wall. After this he gave no further responses.

The experimenter instructed the teacher to continue to shock the learner whether he answered or not. Participants who expressed reservations about their role in the experiment were encouraged to continue by comments such as: 'Please continue', 'You are required to continue'.

Prior to the experiment, Milgram had commissioned the services of an actor. Each participant did not meet another participant but was introduced to the actor instead, who was always given the role of 'learner'. At the briefing both 'participants' received a mild electric shock and were given standard instructions as to how to conduct the experiment. While this was in progress the learner mentioned that he was a war veteran and as a result of his war experiences had a heart problem. What the real participant, the teacher, did not know was that the shock generator was a fake. The learner would only be acting out the part, albeit very convincingly.

RESULTS   Milgram discovered that all of his participants went as far as 300 volts and 65% went the whole way, i.e. to 450 volts.

Prior to the experiment Milgram had asked a panel of 110 experts including 39 psychiatrists how many participants they thought would go as far as 450 volts. These panellists considered that only 10% would be predisposed to continue above 180 volts and few would go the whole way.

Voltage	% of participants refusing to continue the experiment (n = 40)
435–450	65
375–420	2.5
315–360	20
255–300	12.5
195–240	0
135–180	0
75–120	0
15–60	0

As can be seen from the table only a small percentage of participants left the experiment before the dosage became very painful and the learner demanded to be allowed to go. Bearing in mind that the actor had mentioned a health problem this is even more surprising. Of Milgram's 40 participants only 14 refused to continue but only after the dosage had become clearly painful.

DISCUSSION   Milgram expected participants to either refuse to give electric shocks at all or to refuse to carry on once the stooge began to complain. No participant disobeyed the experimenter until 135 volts had been delivered. In addition Milgram noted the number of participants who clearly did not want to harm the 'learner' and did not seem to enjoy inflicting pain, yet continued to administer shocks. He also observed that many were clearly anxious, noting non-verbal behaviour such as stuttering and sweating. As a result of this Milgram believed that obedience to an authority figure was a very potent social force. This study is discussed further in chapter 1.

Article 2

'Effects of group pressure upon the modification and distortion of judgements', S. E. Asch, in H. Guetzkow (ed.) (1951) *Groups, Leadership and Men*, Pittsburgh, PA: Carnegie Press.

AIM   To measure and observe the effects of group pressure.

METHOD   By using a visual stimulus similar to:

target   1   2   3

Asch was able to manipulate group pressure and measure its effects.

Participants in groups of between 7 and 9 were asked to compare the target line with lines 1, 2, 3 and were given the following instructions:

> You see the pair of white cards in front. On the left is a single line; on the right are three lines differing in length. They are numbered 1, 2, 3 in order. One of the three lines at the right is equal to the standard line at the left – you will decide in each case which is the equal line.

A simple enough task you might think. What the participant(s) did not know was that the other 'participants' were in fact confederates of the experimenter and had been instructed to give a false answer in some of the twelve trials. (This is called Asch's standard procedure.) It was arranged also that the true participant was seated near the end of the trial sequence so that they were last or next to last to give their answer. In this way, Asch was able to exert maximum group pressure on his participant, and because it was in a tightly controlled environment it was easier to measure the degree of a participant's readiness to yield to such pressure.

RESULTS   The results from Asch's experimental groups, consisting of 123 naïve male participants, tested on 12 trials, revealed that about one in three participants yielded to group pressure (37%).

VARIATIONS   Asch carried out controlled trials in which naïve participants were allowed to write down their answers in private. In this situation, mistakes were rare; indicating that group influence was minimal.

DISCUSSION   Not all participants conformed and neither did the conforming participants all conform consistently. The range of responses goes from complete independence of the group, in about 25% of the participants, to complete yielding on all twelve trials on the part of 5% of participants. These wide variations indicate that Asch may have been testing aspects of conformity that are more complex than he hypothesised at first.

The study can be criticised on a number of points, e.g. the controls employed. It is worth noting that only men were used and they were all undergraduates at an American university. This is hardly a random sample of society. Similarly the validity of the studies can be questioned in so far as laboratory studies lack ecological validity.

Article 3

Encounter With Unjust Authority, **W. B. Gamson, B. Fireman and S. Rytina (1982), Homewood, IL: Dorsey Press.**

AIM   To study a situation in which participants came to rebel against an authority figure rather than comply with it.

METHOD   Gamson *et al.* conducted a study in which participants were recruited to be involved in research on community standards.

Male and female participants were in groups of 9. Participants were informed that the research was being conducted by an independent company called Manufacturer's Human Relations Consultants (MHRC). When they arrived they were informed that legal disputes often hinge on the idea that there is a community standard of behaviour and that MHRC collected information on this by getting citizens together for group discussion.

The participants then took part in a general questionnaire about themselves and signed a 'participants' agreement'. The latter gave MHRC permission to video their discussions. The person in charge of each group then introduced himself as the 'co-ordinator' and read out the background to a pending court case. This case involved the manager of a garage who was suing an oil company for revoking his franchise, i.e. effectively putting him out of business. The company's case revolved around the assertion that he was living with a woman he was not married to and that his life-style contravened the moral standards of the local community. The company claimed that this meant that he could not maintain good relations with his customers and, therefore, business would suffer. The manager's case hinged on the assertion that the company was out to get him because he had publicly criticised their pricing policy.

After presenting the case, the co-ordinator asked the participants to discuss this while being videotaped. What followed was meant to provoke rebellion:

- The first discussion was stopped, the video was switched off and the co-ordinator asked three participants to argue that the manager's life-style was offensive.
- The second discussion was taped and then stopped, the video was switched off and a further three more participants were instructed to argue against the manager.
- The third discussion was stopped, but this time the group were asked if they would go on video alone and voice their objection to the station manager's affair, say that they would not purchase there any more and state that he ought to lose his franchise.
- In addition they were requested to sign an agreement that gave MHRC the right to edit the tapes and use them as they wished.

RESULTS   As participants began to realise the true intention of MHRC all but 1 of the 33 groups involved in the study began to voice their objections. In 16 groups all members refused to sign the final agreement and in a further 9 only a minority agreed.

DISCUSSION   Their pre-trial questionnaires showed that the majority of the participants were: tolerant of alternative relationships to marriage; considered an employee's private affairs to be none of an employer's business; and were critical of large companies. Many could share this with each other during discussion. In this respect, they were being requested to do something that was against their personal beliefs. As the true intentions of MHRC became more obvious and they realised they would be compromised they rebelled, rather than conforming to being obedient.

Article 4

'Interpersonal dynamics in a simulated prison', C. Haney, C. Banks, and P. G. Zimbardo in *International Journal of Criminology and Penology* (1973) 1, 69–97.

AIM   The purpose of the study was to investigate behaviour in a very structured social environment with clear role expectations, such as a prison.

METHOD   Zimbardo and his colleagues and students created a mock prison in the basement of the Psychology Department of Stanford University in the USA. Twenty-four male, volunteer students were involved in a prison role-play exercise.

After being truthfully informed as to the purpose of the experiment and given personality (Adorno's F-Scale) tests, Zimbardo selected groups of emotionally stable participants all fairly equally matched. On the toss of a coin, one group was assigned to the role of guard (complete with security guard uniform, stick and polarised sunglasses) and the other group was assigned to the role of prisoner. The latter were identified as such by being strip-searched, de-loused and given baggy, nondescript prison clothing with a number on it. The guards were allowed to run the prison how they pleased but were forbidden to physically abuse the prisoners.

The study began with 'prisoners' being arrested unexpectedly by 'guards' at their place of residence. In full view of their neighbours they were handcuffed and taken off in a police car to the mock prison. Zimbardo planned to observe the developing relationship between prisoners and guards over a two-week period but had to stop the study after six days because prisoners were becoming stressed and depressed while the guards were becoming increasingly spiteful and brutal. Guards continually harassed and humiliated prisoners and used psychological techniques to undermine prisoners' confidence, such as making them wear nylon stocking caps, putting them in shackles or waking them in the night to go for role call.

RESULTS   The prisoners for their part initially revolted but soon became docile and passive in the face of the increasing brutality of the guards. In their prison cells they tended to lie around and stare at the ceiling. When they did communicate with each other, it tended to be about prison matters rather than about themselves. Some prisoners had to be released from the study early because they began to show the symptoms of emotional disturbance, e.g. uncontrolled screaming and hysterical crying. One student developed a psychosomatic rash all over his body.

DISCUSSION   In a document presented to a committee on prison reform, Zimbardo (1971) described the effects of the experience on the participants:

> In less than a week, the experience of imprisonment undid (temporarily) a lifetime of learning; human values were suspended, self-concepts were challenged, and the ugliest, most base, pathological side of human nature surfaced.

Article 5

'Patterns of aggressive behaviour in experimentally created "social climates" ', K. Lewin, R. Lippitt and R. K. White in *Journal of Social Psychology* (1939) 10, 271–299.

AIM   Lewin et al. wanted to investigate the effects of different approaches to leadership. In addition they were also interested in observing the patterns of aggression or co-operation within each group, which might result from manipulating the different approach of each leader.

METHOD   They used an after-school hobby club for young boys. There were three groups each with a different type of leader: autocratic, democratic or laissez-faire. Each leader was a confederate of the experimenters and was trained in each style of leadership. The autocratic leader was aloof, strict and task-orientated. The democratic leader was fair and took an interest in each boy's particular project by discussing his ideas with them. The laissez-faire leader had few ideas, left the group to organise themselves and was non-directive.

Each group was organised by each of the confederates behaving in the style assigned to that group but the boys were ignorant of this manipulation. This allowed the researchers to control constitutional aspects such as the individual personalities of each leader. In addition the leaders were rotated after seven weeks until each leader had worked with each group. This was done to further control for any possible extraneous effects that may come from the personality of each leader or the constitution of each group of boys.

RESULTS   The results of the study were:

Leadership style	Effects
Autocratic	were liked less; productivity was high but only when the leader was there; boys were generally aggressive and self-orientated.
Democratic	were liked more; productivity was high whether the leader was there or not; boys were group-centred and friendly.
Laissez-faire	were liked less; productivity was low; boys were group-centred but play-orientated.

DISCUSSION   Lewin *et al.* used the results to popularise the idea that democratic styles of leadership were beneficial in that they encouraged co-operation and work output, whereas the laissez-faire approach produced low productivity and the autocratic approach led to aggression.

Glossary

The first occurrence of each of these terms is highlighted in **bold** type in the main text.

APA is the American Psychological Association, which is responsible for aspects of the science such as the proper conduct of psychological experiments.

agentic state is a term devised by Milgram to describe the condition of being and feeling under the control of an authority figure.

anonymity is a condition in which our identities are unknown to others and is often associated with deindividuation and anti-social behaviour.

anti-conformity is defined as behaviour which is in opposition to group norms.

attribution theory   is concerned with the process whereby we assign a cause to one's own and other's behaviour. The cause is often related to aspects of the environment we find a person in (situational). Alternatively, we say that behaviour is due to constitutional factors, e.g. personality (dispositional).

audience is a group of individuals with a focus of attention, e.g. the way many people turn to look at a stranger.

authoritarian personality is a person predisposed to undemocratic ideals, and behaviour and attitudes associated with it such as ethnocentrism, respect for toughness and submission to authority figures.

autokinetic effect is an optical illusion whereby a stationary spot of light will appear to move in a completely darkened room.

autonomic arousal is what happens to us physiologically when our behaviour changes from a relaxed state to an anxious state and vice versa. These changes can be observed by measuring biological variations in blood pressure or breathing rate.

autonomous state is a term devised by Milgram and is a state of consciousness in which we behave voluntarily and we are aware of our actions and their consequences.

binding forces are elements of a situation that tie the participants psychologically to another's definition of the situation; the other may be a commanding officer or a trainer, for example.

BPS is the British Psychological Society and is responsible for, among other things, the proper conduct of psychological experiments.

collectivism/collectivist refers to cultures where one's role as a person is expressed through relationships and/or the group to which you are attached.

compliance is a term that like conformity is to do with reacting to others. Essentially compliance is the overt behaviour of conforming to the behaviour of others. *See also* conformity.

confabulation is remembering events inaccurately as a result of expectation, elaboration (filling in the gaps) or because the event fits into an already well-established **schema**.

conformity (often confused with obedience) is essentially 'yielding to group pressure' while privately having reservations about your action.

counter-conformity occurs when individuals appear to be in opposition to or reject pressure to conform to group norms.

crowd behaviour is behaviour of a large group of individuals with a common purpose or focus.

defence mechanism is a Freudian concept relating to the way we deal with anxiety-provoking behaviour. Freud maintained that we often deal with anxiety by adopting a pattern of defensive behaviour such as denying that the anxiety, or its cause, is there at all.

deindividuation is a process whereby an individual, as a result of being part of collective action, experiences a loss of identity and therefore loses aspects of themselves such as individual conscience, morality, etc.

demand characteristics are aspects of an experimental procedure which either implicitly or explicitly influence (bias) the behaviour of participants, e.g. because of poor standard instructions participants in the study are invited to respond in a certain way.

denial is a form of defence mechanism whereby the individual refuses to acknowledge the facts as regards to an anxiety-provoking situation.

ecological validity is the extent to which a study, or its procedure, is considered to represent real events outside an experimental laboratory.

ego in Freudian terms, refers to that part of our personality that represents reason and common sense. The ego is unlike the id, which is unorganised, and contains aspects of our behaviour we might refer to as passion. The ego tries to hold the id in check.

enlightenment effect is when the predictions of a psychological theory become so well known they are in danger of influencing the outcome of a study.

ethnocentrism is the tendency to favour all aspects of one's own group.

expectancy effect is a general term used to describe the influence of preconceived beliefs and ideas on social interaction. If I believe that one gender is stronger than the other I may expect to see this in social encounters and in turn this will influence my behaviour in the encounter. *See also* self-fulfilling prophecy.

experimenter effects are an example of demand characteristics. They occur when an experimenter, intentionally or unintentionally, influences the responses of the participants.

foot-in-the-door-technique is an explanation as to why individuals having complied with a minor request, then go on to comply with a more important request.

F-scale is a questionnaire to measure attitudes, namely authoritarianism. Participants have to read statements and say whether they agree/disagree with them. High scorers are thought to be highly prejudicial individuals. *See also* authoritarian personality.

frame of reference is the context and the assumptions within which a social event occurs and which will help to define the event.

fundamental attribution error occurs when we ignore situational causes of behaviour, such as environmental factors, and rely on dispositional causes, e.g. what we think a person is like.

gender (sex) role(s) is behaviour seen as gender specific that is often based on sex and gender stereotypes.

gender stereotypes are over-generalisations about an individual or group, which are based on whether they are male or female. The over-generalisations are often simplistic, fixed and may be negative.

groups are collections of two or more individuals who interact with one another.

group mind is an idea put forward by William McDougall to describe the way people seem to adopt a qualitatively different mode of thinking when a member of a group than when not a member of a group.

group pressure is one aspect of group dynamics whereby an individual tends to change his or her behaviour because of the influence of others.

identification is the process of establishing a link with another person or group which results in taking on the characteristics of that person/group. In Freudian theory this occurs as a form of mental defence. The concept is also used in social learning theory to explain how vicarious reinforcement takes place.

independent behaviour is behaviour that is not responsive to group influences.

individualism/individualist refers to cultures where personal independence and freedom from the opinions of others are encouraged.

individuation is a Jungian concept and essentially is about how we become aware of our own individuality. *See also* deindividuation.

informational influences occur when we accept information supplied by another in order to make sense of our social world.

ingroups are groups of individuals who all feel a strong identity with each other and who tend to act in such a way that others (outgroups) are excluded.

meta-theory is a set of interrelated concepts and principles that help social scientists to define other explanations, i.e. it is a theory about theories.

naturalistic observations are observations made in a natural setting, i.e. not a laboratory.

norm(s)/normative *See* social norms.

obedience (often confused with conformity) is essentially obeying orders or instructions in such a way that you feel a certain amount of compulsion. It is a term that is often used instead of or in addition to compliance.

outgroups are groups of individuals not included in one's own ingroup. The tendency is to perceive them as very different.

personal identity is the sum of the unique characteristics of self that are part of being an individual.

relationship-orientated individuals are group members who are predominantly concerned with group harmony.

role is the part one plays in society, e.g. father, teacher, manager, etc. Most people have multiple roles, e.g. a daughter, a mother and a worker.

role expectations are the attitudes, values and norms we assume go with a particular role in society, e.g. we expect certain type of behaviours from individuals who are teachers or priests.

role orientation is concerned with the fact that social roles bring with them expectations, e.g. leaders are expected to lead whereas subordinates are expected to follow. Some individuals will 'fit' the role expectations ascribed to them more readily than others.

rule orientation is concerned with the fact that some individuals find it difficult to challenge the imposition of rules and regulations. They are often submissive to leaders or other authority figures.

schemas are organised frameworks of knowledge, based on past experience, which help us to interpret and understand current experience.

self-fulfilling prophecy is the idea that an individual's beliefs about another, or group, might elicit from them behaviour that confirms the expectation. In other words, if I believe that an individual or group is lazy this may in turn lead them to exhibit behaviour that confirms my opinion.

self-orientated group members are individuals who are mainly concerned about themselves and are often indifferent to the purposes of the group.

social categorisation is the classification of individuals into various social groups, e.g. male/female, old/young.

social cohesion refers to the social bonds, norms and structure that hold members of a group together over a period of time.

social identity is the part of the self that comes from being a member of various social groups.

social influences are influences on our behaviour that are difficult to attribute solely to say genetic or personality factors. They are associated mainly with individual behaviour in groups.

social norms are accepted ways of behaving that have become the 'norm', i.e. appropriate or normal for a given situation. They are often rooted in sociocultural aspects of a society and tend to help define group membership.

socialisation is a life-long process whereby an individual comes to assimilate the values, norms and social skills that enable them to become fully integrated into a society.

stereotypes are widely shared generalisations about a social group. They are often derogatory images although they can be positive. Stereotyping is the use of these images to describe others.

task-orientated group members are individuals who tend to be more concerned with the goal(s) of the group.

taxonomies are lists or sets of principles used to help classify and arrange phenomena.

totalitarian refers to a system of political rule characterised by centralised power in such a way that most aspects of social life are affected, including education, work, leisure and health.

type and trait theories are theories of personality based on the idea that each of us has a personality largely made up of character traits, such as patience, honesty, keenness, etc. These traits are said to cluster around a basic personality type, such as introversion.

validity is concerned with whether an experiment or procedure for collecting data actually measures or examines what it purports to measure or examine. A study that lacks ecological validity, therefore, is seen as not representing real life.

Bibliography

Abrams, D. and Hogg, M. A. (1990) Social identification, self-categorisation, and social influence, *European Review of Social Psychology*, 1, 195–228.

Adorno, T. W., Frenkel-Brunswik, G., Levinson, D. J. and Sanford, R. N. (1950) *The Authoritarian Personality*, New York: Harper.

Altemeyer, R. A. and Jones, K. (1974) Sexual identity, physical attractiveness, and seating position as determinants of influence in discussion groups, *Canadian Journal of Behavioural Science*, 6, 357–375.

Arendt, H. (1963) *Eichmann in Jerusalem: A Report on the Banality of Evil*, New York: Viking Press.

Argyle, M. (1971) *The Psychology of Interpersonal Behaviour*, Harmondsworth: Penguin.

Aronson, E. (1995) *The Social Animal*, New York: Freeman and Co.

Asch, S. E. (1946) Forming impressions of personality, *Journal of Abnormal and Social Psychology*, 41, 258–290.

—— (1951) Effects of group pressure upon the modification and distortion of judgements, in Guetzkow, H. (ed.) *Groups, Leadership and Men*. Pittsburgh, PA: Carnegie Press.

—— (1952) *Social Psychology*, New York: Holt, Rhinehart and Winston.

—— (1955) Options and social pressure, *Scientific American*, Nov. 31–35.

—— (1956) Studies of independence and conformity: a minority of one against a unanimous majority, *Psychological Monograph*, 70 (9, Whole number 416).

Bales, R. F. and Slater, P. E. (1955) Role differentiation in small decision-making groups, in T. Parsons, R.F. Bales and E.A. Shils (eds) *Family Socialisation and Interaction Process*, New York: Free Press.

Baron, R. A. and Bell, P. A. (1975) Aggression and heat: mediating effects of prior provocation and exposure to an aggressive model, *Journal of Personal and Social Psychology*, 31, 825–832.

Barron, F. (1953) Some personality correlates of independence of judgement, *Journal of Personal and Social Psychology*, 21, 287–297.

Bass, B. M. (1990) *Bass and Stogdill's Handbook of Leadership: Theory, Research and Managerial Applications* (3rd edn), New York: Free Press.

Bavelas, A., Hastorf, A. H., Gross, A. E. and Kite, W. R. (1965) Experiments on the alteration of group structure, *Journal of Experimental Social Psychology*, 1, 55–70.

Benewick, R. and Holton, R. (1987) The peaceful crowd: crowd solidarity and the Pope's visit to Britain, in G. Gaskell and R. Benewick (eds) *The Crowd in Contemporary Britain*, London: Sage.

Bogdonoff, M.D., Klein, E.J., Shaw, M.D. and Back, K.W. (1961) The modifying effect of conforming behaviour upon Lipid responses accompanying CNS arousal, *Clinical Research*, 9, 135.

Browning, C. R. (1992) *Ordinary Men: Reserve Police Battalion 101 and The Final Solution*, HarperCollins.

Bushman, B. J. (1984) Perceived symbols of authority and their influence on compliance, *Journal of Applied Social Science*, 14, 501–508.

Butler, D. and Geis, F. L. (1990) Non-verbal affect responses to male and female leaders: implications for leadership evaluation, *Journal of Personal and Social Psychology*, 58, 48–59.

Carver, C. S. and Scheier, M. F. (1981) *Attention and Self-regulation: A Control Theory Approach to Human Behaviour*, New York: Springer-Verlag.

Chemers, M. M., Hays, R. B., Rhodewalt, F. and Wysocki, J. (1985) A person–environment analysis of job stress: a contingency model explanation, *Journal of Personal and Social Psychology*, 49, 628–635.

Cohen, E. A. (1954) *Human Behaviour in the Concentration Camp*, Cape.

Collins, B. E. and Raven, B. H. (1969) Group structure: attraction, coalitions, communication and power, in G. Lindzey and E. Aronson (eds) *The Handbook of Social Psychology* (2nd edn), Reading, MA: Addison-Wesley.

Crutchfield, R. S. (1954) The measurement of individual conformity to group opinion among officer personnel, Institute of Personal Assessment and Research, University of California, Berkeley, Research Bulletin.

—— (1955) Conformity and character, *American Psychology*, 10, 191–198.

—— (1959) Personal and situational factors in conformity to group pressure, *Acta Psychologica*, 15, 386–388.

Darley, J. M. and Fazio, R. M. (1980) Expectancy confirmation processes arising in the social interaction sequence, *American Psychologist*, 35, 867–881.

Deaux, K., Dane, F. and Wrightsman, L. S. (1988) *Social Psychology*, 6th edn, Pacific Grove, CA: Brooks/Cole Publishing.

Deutsch, M. and Gerard, H. B. (1955) A study of normative and informational social influences upon individual judgement, *Journal of Abnormal and Social Psychology*, 51, 629–636.

Diener, E. (1980) Deindividuation: the absence of self-awareness and self-regulation in group members, in P. B. Paulus (ed.) *Psychology of Group Influences*, Hillsdale, NJ: Erlbaum.

Diener, E., Fraser, S. C., Beaman, A. L. and Kelman, R.T. (1976) Effects of deindividuation variables on stealing by Halloween trick-or-treaters, *Journal of Personal and Social Psychology*, 33, 78–83.

Doms, M. and von Avermaet, E. (1981) Majority influence, minority influence, and conversion behaviour: a replication, *Journal of Experimental Psychology*, 16.

Durkheim, E. (1893) *The Division of Labour in Society*, Glencoe IL: Free Press (1938).

Eitinger, L. and Strøm, A. (1973) *Mortality and Morbidity after Excessive Stress*, Oslo Universitetsforlaget: Humanities Press.

Elms, A. C. (1982) Keeping deception honest: justifying conditions for social scientific research strategies, in T. L. Beauchamps and R. Faden (eds) *Ethical Issues in Social Science Research*, Baltimore, MD: Johns Hopkins University Press.

Evans, R. I. E. (1980) *The Making of Social Psychology: Discussions with Creative Contributors*, Gardner.

Festinger, L., Pepitone, A. and Newcomb, T. M. (1952) Some consequences of deindividuation in a group, *Journal of Abnormal and Social Psychology*, 47, 790–797.

Fielder, F. E. (1965) A contingency model of leadership effectiveness, in L. Berkowitz (ed.) *Advances in Experimental Psychology* (vol. 1), New York: Academic Press.

—— (1971) *Leadership*, Morriston, NJ: General Learning Press.

—— (1981) Leadership effectiveness, *American Behavioural Sciences*, 24, 619–632.

Fleishman, E. A. (1973) Twenty years of consideration and structure, in E. A. Fleishman and J. F. Hunt (eds) *Current Development in the Study of Leadership*, Carbondale. IL: South Illinois University Press.

Freedman, J, R. and Fraser, S.C. (1966) Compliance without pressure: the foot-in-the-door technique, *Journal of Personal and Social Psychology*, 4, 195–202.

French, J. R. P. (1944) Organised and unorganised groups under fear and frustration, *University of Iowa Studies of Child Welfare*, 20, 231–308.

Freud, S. (1921) *Group Psychology and the Analysis of the Ego*, standard edition of the complete works of Sigmund Freud, vol. 18, London: Hogarth Press.

Gamson, W. B., Fireman, B. and Rytina, S. (1982) *Encounter with Unjust Authority*, Homewood, IL: Dorsey Press.

Giddens, A. (1989) *Sociology*, UK: Polity Press.

Gough, H. E. (1960) Theory and measurement of socialisation, *Journal of Consult. Psychology*, 24, 23–30.

Haney, C., Banks, C. and Zimbardo, P. G. (1973) Interpersonal dynamics in a simulated prison, *International Journal of Criminology and Penology*, 1, 69–97.

Heider, F. (1958) *The Psychology of Interpersonal Relations*, New York: Wiley.

Hofling, C. K., Brotman, E., Dalrymple, S., Graves, N. and Pierce, C. M. (1966) An experimental study in nurse–physician relationships, *Journal of Nervous and Mental Diseases*, 143: 171–180.

Hogg, M. A. and Vaughan, G. M. (1995) *Social Psychology: An Introduction*, Hemel Hempstead: Prentice Hall/Harvester Wheatsheaf.

Hollander, E. P. (1985) Leadership and power, in G. Lindzey and E.Aronson (eds) *The Handbook of Social Psychology* (3rd edn), New York: Random House.

Hollander, E. P. and Julian, J. W. (1969) Studies in leader legitimacy, influence, and innovation, in L. Berkowitz (ed.) *Advances in Experimental Social Psychology* (vol. 5), New York: Academic Press.

Holtgraves, T., Srull, T. K. and Socall, D. (1989) The effects of positive self-descriptions on impressions: general principles and individual differences, *Personality and Social Psychology Bulletin*, 15, 452–462.

Hook, S. (1955) *The Hero in History*, Boston: Beacon Press.

Howells, L. T. and Becker, S. W. (1962) Seating arrangements and leadership emergence, *Journal of Abnormal and Social Psychology*, 64, 148–150.

Javornisky, G. (1979) Task content and sex differences in conformity, *Journal of Social Psychology*, 108, 213–220.

Johnson, R. D. and Dowling, L. L. (1979) Deindividuation and valence cues: effects on prosocial and antisocial behaviour, *Journal of Personal and Social Psychology*, 37, 1,532–1,538.

Jung, C. G. (1946) *Psychological Types or the Psychology of Individuation*, New York: Harcourt Brace.

Kelman, H. C. (1958) Compliance, identification, and internalisation, *Journal of Conflict Resolution*, 2, 51–60.

Kelman, H. C. and Hamilton, V. L. (1989) *Crimes of Obedience*, New Haven: Yale University Press.

Kilham, W. and Mann, L. (1974) Levels of destructive obedience as a function of transmitter and executant roles in the Milgram obedience paradigm, *Journal of Personal and Social Psychology*, 29, 696–702.

Krech, D., Crutchfield, R. S. and Ballachey, E. (1962) *Individual in Society*, McGraw-Hill Book Co.

Kruglanski, A. W. (1980) Lay epistemo-logic, process and contents: another look at attribution theory, *Psychology Review*, 87, 70–87.

Kuhn, T. S. (1962) *The Structure of Scientific Revolutions*, University of Chicago Press.

Latané, B. and Nida, S. A. (1981) Ten years of research on group size and helping, *Psychology Bulletin*, 89, 308–324.

Latané, B. and Wolf, S. (1981) The social impact of majorities and minorities, *Psychological Review*, 88, 438–453.

Le Bon, Gustav (1960, reprint of 1895 edn) *The Crowd*, Viking.

Lécuyer, R. (1976) Social organisation and spatial organisation, *Human Relations*, 29, 1,045–1,060.

Levi, P. (1986) *Moments of Reprieve*, Michael Joseph Ltd.

Lewin, K., Lippitt, R. and White, R. K. (1939) Patterns of aggressive behaviour in experimentally created 'social climates', *Journal of Social Psychology*, 10, 271–299.

Lifton, R. J. (1986) *The Nazi Doctors*, Basic.

Loftus, G. R. and Loftus, E. F. (1975) *Human Memory: The Processing of Information*, Halstead Press.

Lord, C. G. (1997) *Social Psychology*, Harcourt Brace College Publishers.

Lovibond, S., Mithrian, H. and Adams, W. G. (1979) The effects of three experimental prison environments on the behaviour of non-convicted volunteer subjects, *Australian Psychologist*, 14, 273–285.

Mann, L. (1981) The baiting crowd in episodes of threatened suicide, *Journal of Personal and Social Psychology*, 41, 703–709.

Manstead, A. and Hewstone, M. (1995) *The Blackwell Encyclopaedia of Social Psychology*, Oxford: Blackwell.

Marsh, P., Rosser, E. and Harré, R. (1978) *The Rules of Disorder*, London: Routledge.

McGregor, D. (1960) *The Human Side of Enterprise*, New York: McGraw Hill.

Milgram, S. (1961) Nationality and conformity, *Scientific American*, 205, 45–51.

—— (1963) Behavioural study of obedience, *Journal of Abnormal and Social Psychology*, 67, 371–378.

—— (1965) Some conditions of obedience and disobedience to authority, *Human Relations*, 18, 57–76.

—— (1974) *Obedience to Authority: An Experimental View*, New York: Harper and Row.

Miller, A. G. (1986) *The Obedience Experiments: A Case Study of Controversy in Social Science*, New York: Praeger.

Nadler, E. B. (1959) Yielding, authoritarianism and authoritarian ideology regarding groups, *Journal of Abnormal and Social Psychology*, 58, 408–410.

Orne, M. T. and Holland, C. C. (1968) On the ecological validity of laboratory deceptions, *International Journal of Psychology*, 6, 282–293.

Perrin, S. and Spencer, C. (1980) The Asch effect: a child of its time?, *Bulletin of the British Psychological Society*, 32: 405–406.

Prentice-Dunn, S. and Rogers, R. W. (1982) Effect of public and private self-awareness on deindividuation and aggression, *Journal of Personal and Social Psychology*, 43, 295–301.

Randle, C. W. (1956) How to identify promotable executives *Harvard Business Review*, 34, 122–134.

Reber, A. S. (1985) *The Penguin Dictionary of Psychology*, Penguin Books: England.

Reicher, S. D. (1987) Crowd behaviour as social action, in J. C. Turner, M. A. Hogg, P. J. Oakes, S. D. Reicher and M. S. Wetherell (eds), *Rediscovering the Social Group: A Self-Categorisation Theory*, Oxford: Blackwell.

Reicher, S. D. and Potter, J. (1985) Psychological theory as inter-group perspective: a comparative analysis of 'scientific' and 'lay' accounts of crowd events, *Human Relations*, 38, 167–189.

Rice, R. W. (1978) Construct validity of the least preferred co-worker score, *Psychological Bulletin*, 85, 1,199–1,237.

Rosenberg, L. A. (1961) Group size, prior experience and conformity, *Journal of Abnormal and Social Psychology*, 63, 436–437.

Rosenhan, D. (1969) Some origins of concern for others, in P. Mussen, J. Langer and M. Covington (eds) *Trends and Issues in Developmental Psychology*, New York: Holt, Rhinehart and Winston.

Rosenthal, R. (1966) *Experimenter Effects in Behavioural Research*, New York: Holt, Rhinehart and Winston.

Rosenthal, R. and Jacobson, L. F. (1968) *Pygmalion in the Classroom*, New York: Holt, Rhinehart and Winston.

Schachter, S. (1951) Deviation, rejection and communication, *Journal of Abnormal and Social Psychology*, 46, 190–207.

Schien, E. H. (1957) Reaction patterns to severe chronic stress in American army prisoners of war of the Chinese, *Journal of Social Issues*, 13, 21–30.

Shanab, M. E. and Yahya, K. A. (1977) A behavioural study of obedience in children, *Journal of Personal and Social Psychology*, 35, 530–536.

Sherif, M. (1935) A study of some social factors in perception, *Archives of Psychology*, 27, 187.

—— (ed.) (1962) *Inter-group Relations and Leadership*, New York: Wiley.

Sherif, M. Harvey, O. J., White, B. J., Hood, W. and Sherif, C. (1961) *Inter-group Conflicts and Co-operation: The Robbers Cave Experiment*, Norman: University of Oklahoma, Institute of Inter-group Relations.

Sistrunk, F. and McDavid, J. W. (1971) Sex variables in conforming behviour, *Journal of Personality and Social Psychology*, 2, 200–07.

Smelser, N. J. (1962) *Theory of Collective Behaviour*, New York: Free Press.

Smith, P. B. and Bond, M. H. (1993) *Social Psychology Across Cultures: Analysis and Perspectives*, London: Harvester Wheatsheaf.

Smith, P. B. and Peterson, M. F. (1988) *Leadership, Organisation and Culture*, London: Sage.

Snyder, M. and Swann, W. B. Jr. (1978) Behavioural confirmation in social interaction: from social perception to social reality, *Journal of Experimental Social Psychology*, 14, 148–162.

Sorrentino, R. M. and Field, N. (1986) Emergent leadership over time: the functional value of positive motivation, *Journal of Personality and Social Psychology*, 50, 1,091–1,099.

Stang, D. J. (1976) Group size effects on conformity, *Journal of Social Psychology*, 98, 175–181.

Staub, E. (1989) *The Roots of Evil: The Origins of Genocide and Other Group Violence*, Cambridge.

Steiner, J. M. (1980) The SS Yesterday and Today: A Sociopsychological View, in J. E. Dimsdale (ed.) *Survivors, Victims, and Perpetrators: Essays in the Nazi Holocaust*, Washington.

Stogdill, R. (1974) *Handbook of Leadership*, New York: Free Press.

Tarde, G. (1903) *The Laws of Imitation*, New York: Holt, Rhinehart and Winston.

—— (1910) *L'Opinion et la foule*, Paris: Alcan.

Turner, R. H. and Killian, L. (1987) *Collective Behaviour* (3rd edn), Englewood Cliffs, NJ: Prentice Hall.

Waddington, D., Jones, K. and Critcher, C. (1987) Flash-points of public disorder, in G. Gaskill and R. Benewick (eds) *The Crowd in Contemporary Britain*, London: Sage.

Weber, M. (1921) *The Theory of Social and Economic Organisation*, New York: Free Press.

Wiesel, E. (1958) *Night*, Les Editions de Minuit.

Wilder, D. (1977) Perceptions of group size, size of opposition and social influence, *Journal of Experimental Social Psychology*, 13, 253–268.

Wolf, S. (1987) Majority and minority influence: a social impact analysis, in M. P. Zanna, J. M. Olson and C. P. Herman (eds) *Social Influence: The Ontario Symposium* (vol. 5), Hillsdale, NJ: Erlbaum (8, 12).

Yukl, G. (1981) *Leadership in Organisations*, Englewood Cliffs, NJ: Prentice Hall.

Zimbardo, P. G. (1970) The human choice: individuation, reason and order versus deindividuation, impulse, and chaos, in W. J. Arnold and D. Levine (eds) *Nebraska Symposium on Motivation 1969* (vol. 17, 237–307), University of Nebraska Press.

—— (1971) The psychological power and pathology of imprisonment. Statement prepared for the US House of Representatives' Committee on the Judiciary, Subcommittee 3: Hearings on Prison Reform, San Francisco: CA.

—— (1973) The psychological power and pathology of imprisonment, in E. Aronson and R. Helmreich (eds) *Social Psychology*, New York: Van Nostrand.

Index